# People Need People

# People Need People

**Bernard J. Weiss**
Reading and Linguistics

**Eldonna L. Evertts**
Language Arts

**Loreli Steuer**
Reading and Linguistics

**Janet Sprout**
Educational Consultant

**Lyman C. Hunt**
General Editor — Satellite Books

Holt
Basic
Reading

Level 9

HOLT, RINEHART AND WINSTON, PUBLISHERS
New York • Toronto • London • Sydney

# Acknowledgments:

*Grateful acknowledgment is made to the following authors and publishers:*

Abelard, Schuman, Publishers, for "Little Wolf," adapted from *Little Wolf* by Ann McGovern. Copyright © 1965 by Ann McGovern. Used by permission.

Coward, McCann & Geoghegan, Inc., for "Christina Katerina and the Box," adapted from *Christina Katerina and the Box* by Patricia Lee Gauch. Copyright © 1971 by Patricia Lee Gauch. Used by permission.

*Cricket,* The Magazine for Children, Vol. 2, No. 8, for "I'll Tell Emily," by Constance Levy. Copyright © 1975 by Constance Levy. Used by permission.

The Dial Press, for "Marvin's Manhole," adapted from *Marvin's Manhole* by Winifred Rosen. Copyright © 1970 by Winifred Rosen. Used by permission.

E. P. Dutton & Co./The Saturday Review Press, for "The Potter and the Tiger," adapted from *It All Began With a Drip-Drip-Drip*, retold by Joan Lexau. Copyright © 1970 by E. P. Dutton & Co./The Saturday Review Press. Used by permission.

Follett Publishing Company and Methuen & Co. Ltd., London, for "Wet Albert," adapted from *Wet Albert* by Michael and Joanne Cole. Copyright © 1967 by Michael and Joanne Cole. Originally published by Methuen & Co. Ltd. Published 1968 in the United States by Follett Publishing Company. Used by permission.

Follett Publishing Company, for "Birthday Gift," from *Farther Than Far* by Margaret Hillert. Copyright © 1969 by Margaret Hillert. For "Angry," from *That Was Summer* by Marci Ridlon. Copyright © 1969 by Marci Ridlon. Used by permission.

Golden Press, division of Western Publishing Company, Inc., for "Pretending," from *Animal Fair* by Alice and Martin Provensen. Copyright © 1962 by Western Publishing Company, Inc. Used by permission.

Harcourt Brace Jovanovich, Inc., for "Others," from *Wizard in the Well* by Harry Behn. Copyright © 1956 by Harry Behn. Used by permission.

Alfred A. Knopf, Inc., for "April Rain Song," from *The Dream Keeper* by Langston Hughes. Copyriht © 1960 by Langston Hughes. Used by permission.

Macmillian Publishing Co., Inc., for "Moodpic," by Estelle Banus. Compiled by Charles E. Schaefer and Kathleen C. Mellor. Copyright © 1971 by Center for Urban Education. Used by permission.

Houghton Mifflin Company, for "Tammy Camps in the Rocky Mountains," adapted from *Tammy Camps in the Rocky Mountains* by Mary Elizabeth Baker. Copyright © 1970 by Mary Elizabeth Baker. Used by permission.

William Morrow & Co., Inc., for "Quiet on Account of Dinosaur," adapted from *Quiet on Account of Dinosaur* by Jane Thayer. Copyright © 1964 by Catherine Woolley. Used by permission.

Parents' Magazine Press, for "Junk Day on Juniper Street," adapted from *Junk Day on Juniper Street* by Lilian Moore. Copyright © 1969 by Lilian Moore. For "Maxie," adapted from *Maxie* by Mildred Kantrowitz. Copyright © 1970 by Mildred Kantrowitz. For "Boy, Was I Mad!" adapted from *Boy, Was I Mad!* by Kathryn Hitte. Copyright © 1969 by Kathryn Hitte. Used by permission.

Random House, Inc., and International Creative Management, for "Giraffe! Giraffe!" by Hipolito Rivera on p. 133 from *Rose, Where Did You Get That Red? Teaching Great Poetry to Children* by Kenneth Koch. Copyright © 1973 by Kenneth Koch. Used by permission.

Russell & Volkening, Inc., as agents for Mary Ann Hoberman, for "Wish" by Mary Ann Hoberman. Copyright © 1974 by Mary Ann Hoberman. Used by permission.

Van Nostrand Reinhold Company, for "Freddy Found a Frog," adapted from *Freddy Found a Frog* by Alice James Napjus. Copyright © 1969 by Alice James Napjus. Used by permission.

# Art Credits:

# Photo Credits:

# Table of Contents

## UNIT TWO
# THINKING OF OTHERS

# WHAT WOULD YOU DO?

## I'll Tell Emily

I'm going to pet a worm today
I'm going to pet a worm—don't *say*
Don't pet a worm, I'm doing it soon—
Emily's coming this afternoon!
And you know what she'll probably say
*I touched a mouse* or
*I held a snake* or
*I felt a dead bird's wing*
And she'll turn to me with a kind of smile
*What did you do that's interesting?*
This time
I am
Going to say
*Why, Emily, you should have seen*
*me pet a worm today!*
And I'll tell her he stretched and
he shrunk like elastic
And I got a chill and it felt fantastic
And I'll see her smile fade away when she
Wishes that moment she could be me!

*Constance Levy*

Alice James Napjus

# Freddy Found a Frog

**PART ONE**

## What Do You Do With a Frog?

Freddy made a small boat. He put it
in some water to see if it would go. He put
a small stone in the boat for one man. He put in
a big stone for another man. But when
he put in another stone, it was too much.

Down dropped the boat. Down and down
it went.

Freddy put his hand way down in the water
to get the boat. He found something, but it wasn't
his boat. It was a frog. A big green frog!

"What a beautiful frog!" said Freddy.

The frog may have heard Freddy because it said,

"Croak, croak."

Freddy jumped.
Then the frog jumped.
It jumped right out of Freddy's hands!

"Frog, where are you?" asked Freddy.

Croak

There it was, right near Freddy's hand.
Freddy wasn't going to let the frog get away
this time. He picked it up.

"This isn't a good place for you," said Freddy.
"I'm going to find a home for you."

He put the frog into his pocket and walked
up the street.

As Freddy walked, he began to sing.
Now and then the frog would help him out
by saying,

Freddy stopped when he saw Mr. Mays.
But Freddy didn't take his hand from his pocket.
  "Good morning," said Freddy. Then he asked,
"Mr. Mays, what would you do with a frog?"

"I don't have a frog," said Mr. Mays. "But if I did, I would take it fishing."

Freddy laughed. "Frogs can't fish," he said.

"No, no," said Mr. Mays. "The frog would be my bait. I would drop it into the water. The fish would see it. The frog would help me get the fish."

The frog gave a jump in Freddy's pocket.

"Bait!" said Freddy. "No, no. Not my frog!"

Freddy ran off with the frog under his hand. His frog was not going to be fishing bait.

Mr. Mays looked as Freddy ran off. "Now what did I say to make him do that?" he thought.

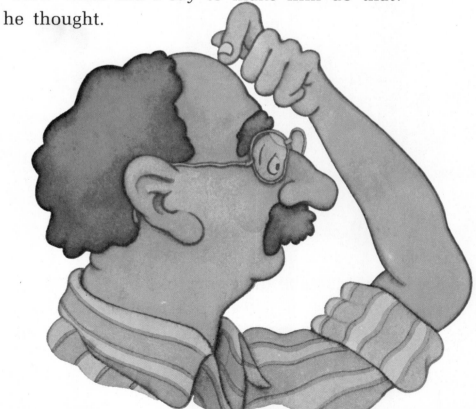

# The Best Place

Freddy didn't stop running. He ran
and ran. He ran with his hand in his pocket.
He didn't want to drop his frog.

Then Freddy met Miss Denny. She was coming
home from work. Everyone said that Miss Denny
was wise. She might know what to do with a frog.

"Hello, Freddy," said Miss Denny.

"Hello, Miss Denny," said Freddy. "May I
ask you something? If you had a frog,
what would you do with it?"

"If I had a frog," said Miss Denny, "I know
just what I'd do. I'd cook it. Frog legs
are very good to eat."

When Freddy heard that, he began to run
again. He wanted to get home. The frog gave
a little jump in Freddy's pocket.

"It's all right, little frog," said Freddy.
"I'll take you home. I'll find a good place
for you there."

Freddy found his mother. She was in back
of their home. Freddy didn't say anything
for a long time. He just looked at her.

At last he said, "Mother, what would you do
if you had a frog?"

"If I had a frog, I'd put it in my little pond.
That's the best place for a frog, Freddy," said Mother.

Freddy put his hand in his pocket,
and the frog gave another little jump.
"It's all right, frog," he said. "I found
a good home for you."

Freddy ran to the pond and let the frog jump
out of his hand and into the pond.
Then Freddy saw the frog jump up onto
a big white flower in the middle of the pond.
It looked very green, sitting there
on the white flower.

Just then Freddy's mother came over to the pond.

"Look, Mother," said Freddy. "My frog likes
its new home. Isn't it beautiful?"

"Yes, Freddy," Mother said. "It is."

And Freddy's frog said,

"Croak."

# What's the Question?

Sentences that start with words like *who, what, where,* and *when* are almost always questions.

> *Who* is that?
> *What* day is it?
> *Where* do you live?
> *When* are we going home?

Finish these sentences. Will your sentences tell something or ask something?

> Who ___ ___ ___?
> What ___ ___ ___?
> Where ___ ___ ___?
> When ___ ___ ___?

**Question Markers.** Have the sentence at the top of the page and the questions below it read and discussed. Note the italicized words. Then let the children make up questions by filling in the blanks.

Patricia Lee Gauch

# Christina Katerina and the Box

Christina Katerina liked boxes. Best of all she liked big boxes. She liked the one that the new TV came in.

"It's just beautiful!" Christina's mother said. She was looking at the TV.

"It is! It is!" said Christina. She was looking at the TV box.

Christina put the box under the apple tree. Mother thought it would be best to throw out the box. But she said Christina could put it under the apple tree for a day or two.

Christina's father put a window and a door
in the box. Christina painted a tower on the box.
And the box was . . . a castle. She put her
toy bears and some cookies in the castle.

For two days Christina and her bears lived
and played in the castle.

Then Watson came over. Watson was
Christina's friend. He got into the castle when
Christina was out. He ate all her cookies.
Christina locked him in because he ate
her cookies. She made him say, "I'm sorry,"
ten times.

At last Christina let him out. Watson
had not liked being locked in the castle.
He gave Christina's castle a kick.
Over it went, tower and all.

"That takes care of your castle," said Mother.
She began to take it away.

"But that's no castle," said Christina.
"That's my clubhouse!"

And it was . . . for three long days.

Christina made the door into a window.
She made the window into a door.
Then she painted a lock on the door.
She put up a sign that said, "Club."
She asked Watson to be part of the club.

Christina and Watson sat in the clubhouse. They ate. They talked. Christina and Watson said they would be friends. And they were.

They were friends until Watson wanted to be head of the club. Watson climbed onto the clubhouse. He said he would sit there until Christina made him head of the club.

But the clubhouse caved in.

"That takes care of your clubhouse,"
said Mother. She began to take it away.

"But that's my racing car. And I'm going
to a race."

Before taking off, Christina put on
her racing hat. She painted lights on the car.
For two days she "raced" up and down
under the apple tree. She won every time.

Then Watson said that the car didn't
run right. He would look at it.
Watson sawed a hole in the car to look.
But the car fell apart.

"That takes care of your racing car," said Mother. She began to take it away.

"But that's no racing car," said Christina. "That's my new dance floor. And I'm going to have a dance."

And she did, right there under the apple tree.

Christina opened the box out flat and painted flowers on it. Then she and her bears and Watson put on their best coats and hats. They asked everyone to come to the dance. And everyone came and danced and danced.

27

They danced until Watson said the floor
had to be mopped. He put water on the floor
and mopped and mopped. But the dance floor
fell apart.

"That takes care of your floor," said Mother.
"What floor?" asked Christina.
"That flat old box? Let's throw it away."

At last Mother could take it away.

"But look . . . ," said Christina Katerina. "Watson found two boats just now. I said we could play with them right here under the apple tree. I said my mother wouldn't care at all."

S.S. CHRISTINA

S.S. WATSON

Ann McGovern

# LITTLE WOLF

## PART ONE
## Not a Hunter

It is morning. The sun is in the sky.
It shines on the houses of the Indian tribe.

The sun shines on the mother, Flower Wolf.
It shines on the father, Hunt Wolf.
It shines on the grandfather, Wise Wolf.
And the sun shines on the boy, Little Wolf.

Another day has come. Flower Wolf will work
at home. Hunt Wolf will hunt in the forest.
Wise Wolf will sit by the fire.

Little Wolf will go into the forest.
But Little Wolf will not hunt.
This will not please Hunt Wolf.

Little Wolf will not hunt like other boys.
He is not a hunter. He finds animals
that cannot run. He finds birds that
cannot fly. Little Wolf takes them home.
He makes them well again.

Today Hunt Wolf wants Little Wolf to hunt.
"Today you will please me," says Hunt Wolf.
"Today you will hunt."

Little Wolf only looks at his father.

"You are brave," says Hunt Wolf to his son.
"But what good is it to be brave?
You will not kill the bear!"

Then Hunt Wolf says, "You can run fast.
You can run as fast as other boys.
But what good is it? You will not run
and catch the rabbit.

"You are wise. You know the ways
of the forest. But what good is it?
You will not trick the fox.

"You are brave. You are fast.
You are wise. But what good is it?
You will not hunt."

Wise Wolf hears all that Hunt Wolf says.
"We kill animals to eat," says Wise Wolf.
"We could not live if we did not hunt.
But Little Wolf will not hunt.
So let the boy be."

"NO!" says Hunt Wolf. "My son will hunt.
Go now, Little Wolf! Go into the forest.
Come back when you kill a bear or a rabbit
or a fox."

So Little Wolf walks off. He walks
by houses of the other Indians.
He walks by the Chief's house. He
sees the Chief's only son, Brave Bear.
Now Brave Bear is only a small boy.
But one day he will be a brave hunter.

Little Wolf looks at the Chief and
Brave Bear. He says, "Good morning."
But they do not say a thing to him.
Little Wolf is not a hunter. He is not
like the other boys in the tribe.

Little Wolf goes into the forest.
Everything is very green.
Everything is very quiet.

Little Wolf knows the forest well.
Wise Wolf, his grandfather, showed him
the ways of the forest. Wise Wolf showed
him the ways of the animals and the plants.

Little Wolf knows that some plants
make people sick. He knows that
some plants make people well, too.

Soon Little Wolf sees a small, white tail.
It is the white tail of a rabbit.

Little Wolf looks at the rabbit.
"How can I be a hunter?" he asks.
"How can I be a hunter if I have to kill you?"

The rabbit runs off. Soon it is gone.

Little Wolf sees two big eyes.
He sees the eyes of a fox.
Little Wolf looks into the eyes.

"I will not kill you," says Little Wolf.
"I will not hunt if I have to kill you."

Then Little Wolf sees the tail of a fox.
He sees that it is in a trap. Little Wolf
opens the trap. The fox runs free.

"I will not kill animals," says Little Wolf.
"I will not be a hunter."

PART TWO
# A Healer

Now it is night. The moon is in the sky.
It shines on the houses of all the Indians.

The moon shines on the mother, Flower Wolf.
It shines on the father, Hunt Wolf.
It shines on the grandfather, Wise Wolf.
And the moon shines on the boy, Little Wolf.

It is time for Little Wolf to go home.
The animals and the plants are sleeping.
Little Wolf wants to go to sleep, too.
But he will not have a thing to show Hunt Wolf.
No bear! No rabbit! No fox!
Still Little Wolf will go home.

In the dark, quiet forest there is a noise.
"That is not a noise of the forest,"
thinks Little Wolf. He is very still.
He looks about him. He knows that he is
near the noise. Then he finds Brave Bear.
And Brave Bear sees him.

"I am very sick," says Brave Bear.
"I may not live. Run for help.
Run for my father."

Little Wolf sees some berries. He knows
the berries. They make people sick.

"Did Brave Bear eat the berries?"
thinks Little Wolf. "That's it.
The berries made him sick."

Then Little Wolf says, "There is no time
to run for help. You need help right now.
I can heal you."

"You?" Brave Bear says. "What can you do?
You cannot hunt or kill animals."

"I know the ways of the forest," Little Wolf
says. "I can heal you."

Little Wolf picks up some plants.
"Eat these plants," he says.
"They will make you well.
You will be well when the sun shines again."

All night Little Wolf sits by Brave Bear.
The two boys sleep in the forest.
The forest is very quiet.
The moon shines on the boys.

It is morning again. The moon is gone.
The sun is in the sky. It shines on the boys.
It shines on them as they walk home.

Brave Bear goes home with Little Wolf.
He tells about the way Little Wolf
healed him. Hunt Wolf says not a thing.
He sits and thinks.

Then Hunt Wolf says, "It is good
that you are well, Brave Bear. We need you.
Some day you will be a great Chief.
And you will be a great hunter."

Then Hunt Wolf looks at his son.
"We need you, too, Little Wolf. Some day
you will be a great healer."

This day Flower Wolf will work in the house.
Hunt Wolf will hunt in the forest.
Wise Wolf will sit by the fire.
And Little Wolf will go into the forest.

Little Wolf will not kill the animals.
No bear! No rabbit! No fox!

But he will see the animals.
And he will find out about them.

He will see plants in the forest.
He will find out about them, too.

And that is Little Wolf's way.

# Helping Others

Who helps you keep well? People! The people you see on these pages work in the *health services.*

Look at these pictures. Can you tell who's who? How does each of these people help you keep well?

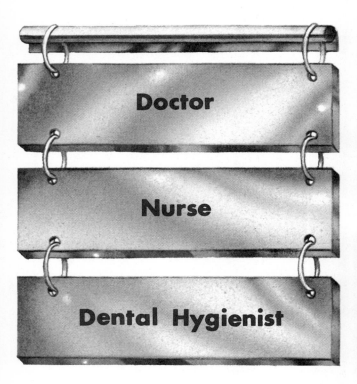

Doctor

Nurse

Dental Hygienist

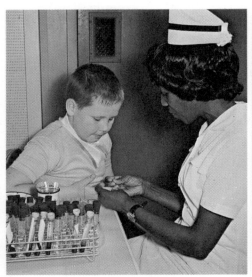

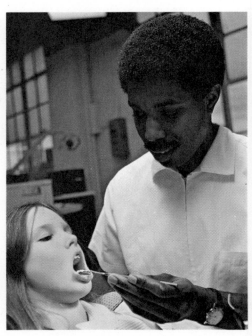

# Pharmacist

This man is a *pharmacist.* He prepares and sells the medicine that the doctor or dentist asks for. What special skills do you think a pharmacist should have?

# Medical Technician

This man is a *medical technician.* He works in a hospital. Here you see him looking at some blood samples. How do you think the microscope helps the medical technician do his work?

These are just some of the people who work to keep you well. Do you know any others?

43

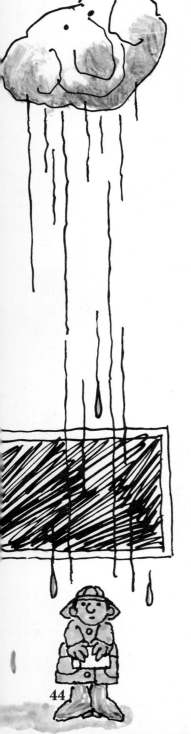

Michael and Joanne Cole

# Wet Albert

PART ONE

## The Cloud

Clouds come, and clouds go.
But there was one cloud that came
and didn't go. It came
floating along in the sky one day
and stopped over a little boy
called Albert. And it rained.

The cloud went everywhere with Albert.
And everywhere they went, it rained.
When Albert went to the park
with his sister, the two of them had
to play in the rain.

When Albert went for a walk
with his mother, she got wet, too.
And when Albert went to school, he got
the room all wet. Albert was asked
to do his schoolwork at home.

When Wet Albert was home, so much rain came down on his house that in no time at all there was water all over the house. Wet Albert and his mother and father and sister had to climb on top of the house.
When the water got to the top of the house, they all had to jump onto a bed that came floating out of Albert's room. The bed went floating along with Albert and his family.
In time they came to a river.

"Let's live on the river!" said Wet Albert.

"On a bed, Albert?" asked his mother.

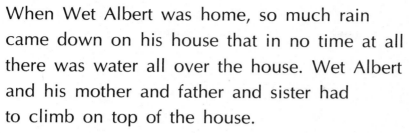

"No, on a boat!" said his father. "Good idea! A little rain on the river will be all right."

So Wet Albert's family set up house on an old boat.
Wet Albert's father got him a little boat of his own.
Whenever anyone wanted to sit in the sun,
Albert would go off alone on his boat and fish.

Albert's father had to have work,
so he thought about what he could do
on the river. Then he got an idea.
He could take things from place to place
along the river — pigs, cows, clothes, flowers, books.
Everything and anything! He could bring people
whatever they wanted. And that is what he did.

"This is the life," said Wet Albert's father.
"This is the life."

And the days went by like the trees along the river.

PART TWO

# The Drought

That summer there was a drought in the town
where Wet Albert had lived. Day after day
went by with no rain. The sun had dried up all the rivers.
All but Wet Albert's! It was
the only river that had water.
Wet Albert and his family were
still floating up and down the river
in their boat.

Life was good for Wet Albert and his family.
But not for the people in the little town!
Because of the drought, not a thing would grow.
How could anything grow without rain?

There was very little for the people and animals
to eat. And there wouldn't be anything to eat
all that winter if there was no rain
to help things grow.

It was lucky that there was one cloud in the sky that summer. And that cloud was Wet Albert's!

"Let's get Wet Albert to help us," said the farmers. "If he comes to our farms, he will bring rain."

Wet Albert was happy to help the farmers. He went to all the farms. And wherever he went, the rain from his cloud made the farms green. Things began to grow again.

Then Albert went to all the rivers, and his rain cloud put water back into them.

Thanks to Wet Albert there was a harvest that fall.
And a good harvest, too! The farmers took
some of it to Wet Albert and his family.

People around the world heard the news
of Wet Albert. Wherever there was a drought,
people would say, "Get Wet Albert!"

But how could he get to places around the world?

One man had a good idea. "Get the boy
a helicopter," he said. "Then he can bring
rain to everyone."

So Wet Albert got a helicopter of his own.
He went all over the world bringing rain
wherever there was a drought.

But after every trip, he was happy to come back to his family on the old boat.

"Nothing like a drop of rain to make the place look like home again," said Albert's father.

After that, Albert had the helicopter right there on the boat with him. Then he could take off right away if there was another drought.

Clouds come, and clouds go.
But if you ever see a cloud come and go with a helicopter under it, you'll know that there is a drought somewhere. And Wet Albert is on his way with rain.

# April Rain Song

Let the rain kiss you.
Let the rain beat upon your head
    with silver liquid drops.
Let the rain sing you a lullaby.
The rain makes still pools
    on the sidewalk.
The rain makes running pools
    in the gutter.
The rain plays a little sleep-song
    on our roof at night—
And I love the rain.

—Langston Hughes

53

# Rumpelstiltskin

## part one

An old man had a very beautiful daughter.
One day the old man went to see the king.
He wanted to let the king know that he was
someone special. When the king came into the room,
the old man said, "I have a daughter who can
spin gold out of straw."

"You have?" said the king. "If your daughter can
spin gold out of straw, I'd like to see her.
Bring her to me in the morning, and I will see
what she can do."

54

So the next day the old man came to the castle
with his daughter. The king took the girl
to a small room that had lots of straw.
Then the king said, "Now get to work. I want you
to spin this straw into gold tonight.
I'll come back in the morning to get the gold."

The girl sat alone in the room. She didn't know
how to spin straw into gold, and she began to cry.

Just then the door opened, and a funny-looking
little man came in. "Hello," he said.
"Why are you crying?"

"The king wants me to spin gold out of this straw by tonight, and I don't know how to do it," said the girl.

The little man asked, "What will you give me if I spin it for you?"

"I'll give you this little gold mirror," said the girl.

The little man took the mirror, sat down, and began to spin the straw. He worked all night, and by morning he had made gold out of all the straw.

When the king came into the room in the morning, he was very happy to see all the gold. He took the old man's daughter to another room that had lots of straw. The king told the girl to spin the straw into gold that night.

When the girl saw all that straw, she began to cry again. She still didn't know how to spin straw into gold.

The door opened, and the same little man came in. "What will you give me this time if I spin the straw into gold for you?" he asked the girl.

"I'll give you my ring," she said.

The little man took the ring and sat down and began to spin the straw. By morning he had made gold out of all the straw.

The king came into the room the next morning and was very happy to see all the gold. He took the girl to a very big room that had lots of straw. The king told her to spin all the straw into gold. "If you can spin all this straw into gold by morning, you will be my queen," he said.

When the girl was alone, the little man came into
the room again. And again he asked,
"What will you give me if I spin the straw for you?"

"I don't have anything to give you," said the girl.

"If you become queen and have a child, give me
the child," said the little man.

The girl saw no other way to get help.
So she said she would give the little man
what he asked. The man sat down to spin. He worked
all night, and by morning he had made gold
out of all the straw.

# PART TWO

When the king came into the room in the morning,
he found all the gold he could ever want.
"You will be my queen," he said to the girl.
"And you will not have to spin straw ever again."
So the next day the old man's daughter became a queen.

Some time after that, the king and queen had
a beautiful child. The queen was so happy, she forgot
all about the funny-looking little man. But one day
the door to her room opened, and there he was.

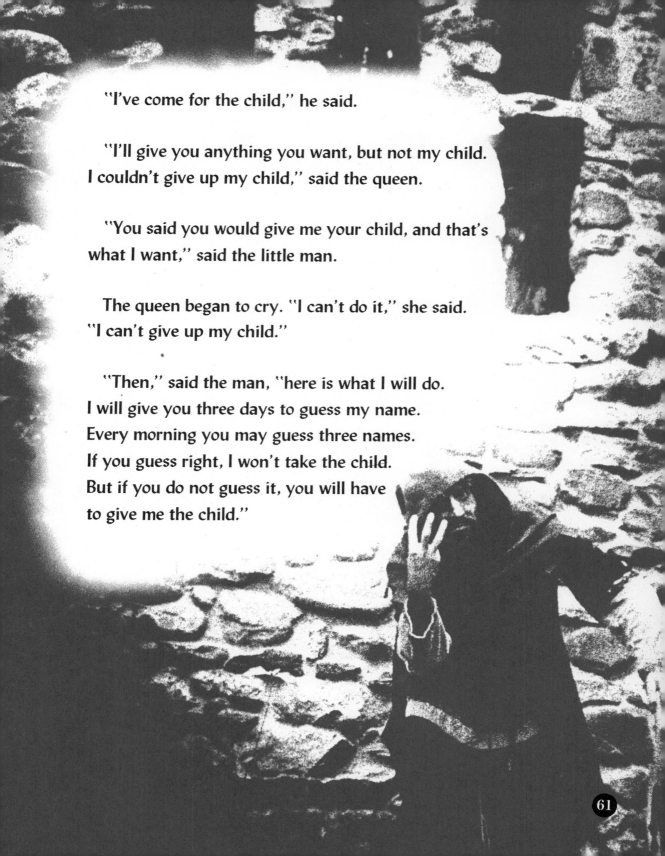

"I've come for the child," he said.

"I'll give you anything you want, but not my child. I couldn't give up my child," said the queen.

"You said you would give me your child, and that's what I want," said the little man.

The queen began to cry. "I can't do it," she said. "I can't give up my child."

"Then," said the man, "here is what I will do. I will give you three days to guess my name. Every morning you may guess three names. If you guess right, I won't take the child. But if you do not guess it, you will have to give me the child."

That night the queen thought of every name
she had ever heard. Then she called her page
and told him to go out and find other names.

In the morning when the little man came to the castle,
the queen tried to guess his name.

"Is your name Mr. Appleflower?" she asked.

"No," said the little man.

"Is it Mr. Greenpot?" asked the queen.

"No," said the man.

"Is it Mr. Crabtree?" she asked.

"No," said the little man. "You didn't guess it.
I'll be back in the morning, and you can try again."

The next day the queen asked for names from people who lived near the castle. When the little man came to the castle, the queen tried to guess his name again.

"Is your name Mr. Birdwing?" she asked.

"No," said the little man.

"Is it Mr. Whitecoat?" she asked.

"No," he said.

"Is it Mr. Tigerbutton?" she asked.

"No," he said. "You can try again in the morning." And with that the man was gone.

On the last day the page ran to the queen. "I found
a new name," he said. "In a house in the forest,
a funny-looking little man was singing.
He was singing about a queen's child and how lucky
he was that no one would know his name was
Rumpelstiltskin."

The queen was very happy when she heard the name
Rumpelstiltskin. She thanked the page and went
to her room to wait for the little man.

When the little man came to the castle, he said, "Can you guess my name today?"

"Is your name Mr. Goodfish?" the queen asked.

"No," said the man.

"Is it Mr. Pennypond?" she asked.

"No," he said.

"Could it be Rumpelstiltskin?" asked the queen.

The little man began jumping up and down. "How did you guess?" he cried.

But the queen wouldn't tell him. She called her page and told him to take the man away.

And that was the last anyone ever saw of the funny-looking little man.

# What Things Could Really Happen?

The stone is floating on the water.
Brad is running as fast as his kitten.

My brother painted our house red.
I will turn this bean into an apple.

Rosa's dog can swim in the pond.
My pet camel goes everywhere I go.

Tonight I'll fly to the moon and back.
This afternoon my family is going
to the park.

**Fantasy and Reality.** Have the children read each pair of sentences, then discuss
which event could really happen and which is make-believe.

# THINKING
## OF OTHERS

### Others

Even though it's raining
I don't wish it wouldn't.
That would be like saying
I think it shouldn't.
I'd rather be out playing
Than sitting hours and hours
Watching rain falling
In drips and drops and showers,
But what about the robins?
What about the flowers?

—Harry Behn

Mildred Kantrowitz

# maxie

## PART ONE
## Every Day the Same

Maxie lived all alone. She lived
in three small rooms. The rooms were
in an old brownstone house. Maxie
had lived there a long time. Every day
was the same for her.

Every morning at 7:00, up went the shades
on Maxie's living room windows. At 7:10
Maxie's cat ran to the middle window.
He sat and looked at the street.

At 7:20 the shade on the back window
went up. At 7:22 Maxie gave her bird
some water and seeds. Then the bird began
to sing. Everyone knew it was 7:22.

At 8:15 Maxie's door opened. Maxie walked down five sets of stairs. She walked down to get her newspaper. She would try to hold the door open with one foot. Then she would reach out to get the newspaper. Every morning Maxie would reach just a little too far. Her foot would not hold the door. The door always closed. And Maxie couldn't get back in.

So at 8:20 Maxie always had to ring for Walter to let her in. Walter knew it was Maxie. He would open the door. Maxie would come in with her newspaper.

At 8:45 every morning, Maxie made a pot of tea.
She put on the teakettle. All the people
in the brownstone heard the teakettle whistle.
How Maxie loved that whistle! She let it sing
for a long time. Dogs and cats would sing with it.
Then the whistle would stop. The people would know
it was 8:46 then. And it always was.

The mail carrier knew Maxie best. He knew
she had a sister. He knew where the sister
lived. He saw Maxie's mail from her. He knew
when Maxie put seeds in her window boxes.
The seeds came in the mail.

Every morning at 9:00, Maxie walked
down five sets of stairs again. This time
she went to see the mail carrier. At 9:00
he came with the mail. Maxie picked up her mail.
Then she climbed back up the five sets of stairs.
When she got to her floor, she went
into her apartment. The door closed after her.

# Who Needs Maxie?

It was Monday afternoon. At 1:05
Maxie moved her bird to the living room.
Maxie moved the bird every afternoon at 1:05.
Then the cat moved to the back window.
And soon it was asleep.

"You're happy when you're asleep. You sleep
by the window all the time," Maxie said
to the cat. "All you want to do is sleep.
First in one window, then in the other.
You don't need anyone. And no one needs you.
But you don't care."

Maxie walked away from the window. "I care,"
she said. Maxie went to bed.

That was Monday.

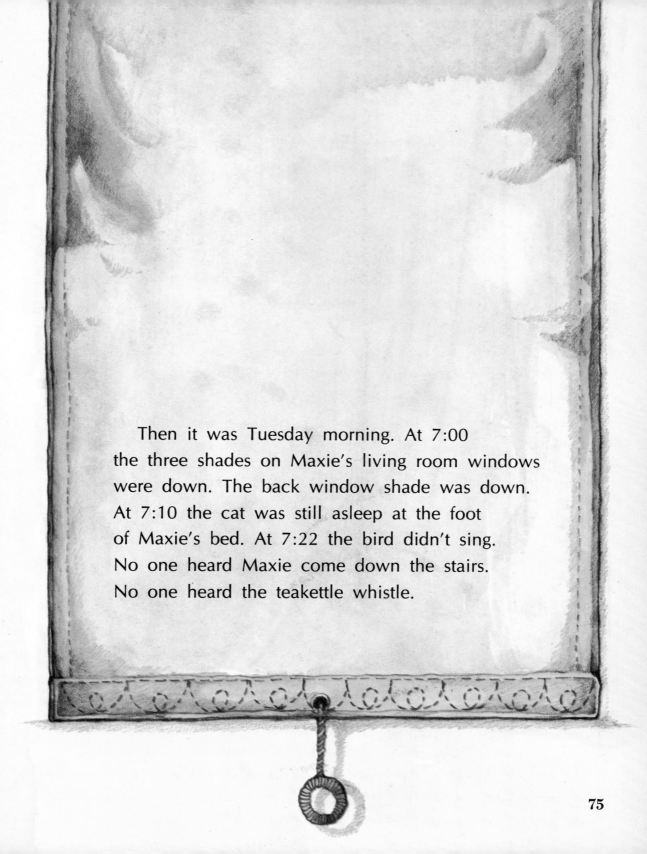

Then it was Tuesday morning. At 7:00
the three shades on Maxie's living room windows
were down. The back window shade was down.
At 7:10 the cat was still asleep at the foot
of Maxie's bed. At 7:22 the bird didn't sing.
No one heard Maxie come down the stairs.
No one heard the teakettle whistle.

75

At 9:00 the mail carrier came. He had
seeds for Maxie. He waited for her to come
down the stairs. When she didn't come,
he became upset. He climbed the five sets
of stairs to Maxie's apartment. Then he called
her name. He waited. But no one came
to the door.

At 9:03 a man who lived in the brownstone
came up the stairs. At 9:05 Mrs. Greenhouse
came up the stairs. At 9:07 Mrs. Stone came
from next door. Penny Parks came up at 9:10
with her brothers. Walter was the last one
to come up. By that time it was 9:17.
All of the people were upset. They were waiting
for Maxie to open the door.

When Maxie didn't open the door, Walter
opened it. All of the people went in. They
found Maxie in bed. Someone called a doctor.
The doctor came right away. She went
into Maxie's bedroom and closed the door.

When the doctor came out, she said, "Maxie isn't sick. She's lonely. She doesn't feel loved. She doesn't feel that anyone needs her."

No one said a thing.

Then Mrs. Stone walked into the bedroom. "Maxie!" she said. "You and that bird let Mr. Stone down. Every morning when the bird sings, Mr. Stone gets out of bed. The bird didn't sing this morning. Mr. Stone didn't get up. He's still sleeping. Now he won't be on time for work. All because of you and that bird!"

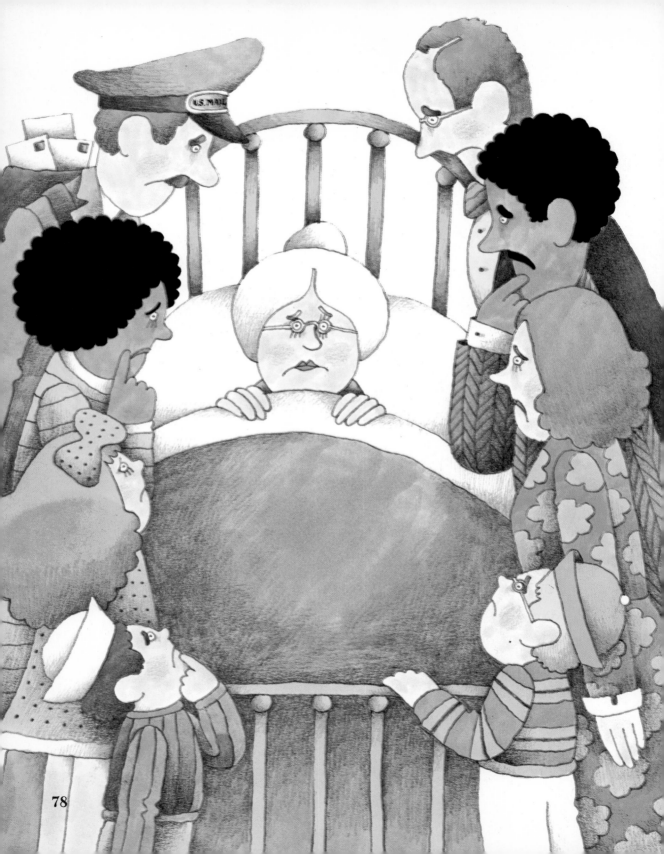

All the people went into the bedroom.
They told Maxie how much they needed her.
Penny Parks did not get up on time for school.
She did not hear the teakettle whistle.
Mr. and Mrs. Greenhouse did not get up.
They did not see Maxie's shades go up.
Walter did not get up to paint an apartment.
Maxie did not ring for him to let her in.

Maxie found out how much people needed her.
Maxie was happy. She got out of bed.
She put on the teakettle. She made a pot of tea.
By 9:45 everyone had gone. Maxie went
to the window boxes. She began to plant
the seeds that had come in the mail.

# *Junk Day on Juniper Street*

Lilian Moore

No one on Juniper Street can really say
how it all began. Ben and Jenny say it began
in their house. Sandy says it really began
in her backyard. Mike says it began with his father.
Mike may be right.

One day Mike's father was reading
his newspaper. "Take a look at this!"
he said. "Are they talking about us?"

**Do you have junk around your house?
Then it's clean-up time!**

"Do we have junk?" asked Mike.
"*Hmmmm . . . ,*" said his mother.

Then Mike's mother saw Sandy and her mother in the backyard. Mike's mother said, "Look at this." She showed Sandy's mother the newspaper.

"Do we have junk?" asked Sandy.
"*Hmmmm . . .*" said her mother.

Some mothers went to Ben and Jenny's house for tea. "Did you see this?" asked Sandy's mother. And she showed them the newspaper.

Jenny asked, "Do we have junk?"

All the mothers laughed. "We all have junk," they said. "Lots and lots of junk!"

Then someone said, "Let's do it! Let's have a Take-Out-All-the-Junk Day!"

So Juniper Street had a Junk Day.

It was clean-up time in every house.
People walked from one room to the next.
They said, "Do we really need this?"

Then people began to put their junk
out on the street. There were old beds
and old clothes. There were old toys
and pictures and books.

Still people looked around their houses.
And they saw other things to take out.
There was an old radio. There was
a big old rocking chair.

In no time at all, there was junk by every house on Juniper Street. Mike's father looked up and down the street. "We're going to need a big truck to pick up all this junk!"

So Ben's father called up the junk man. "We have lots of junk on Juniper Street," he told the man. "You will need a big truck to take it all away."

"I have a big truck," said the junk man. "But I can't come today. I will come for your junk in the morning."

"Don't forget," said Ben's father, "a big truck."

All day people walked by the junk
on Juniper Street. No one could go by
WITHOUT looking at the junk.

Mike stopped at Sandy's house.
"Say," he said. "There's a good saw.
I need a saw like that to make my treehouse.
May I have it?"

Sandy's mother said yes.

Sandy's father stopped to look at the junk by Mike's house. He saw an old box. "Why, it's just what I need!" he said.

"Take it!" said Mike's father.

Jenny's mother saw a big table she liked. "I need a table like that to work on," she said. "There's so much to do at the newspaper. Sometimes I have to work at home."

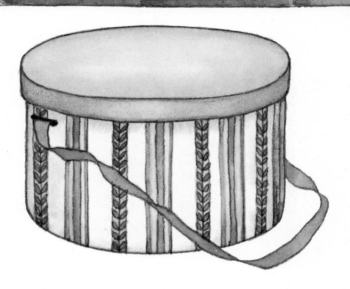

Sandy's mother found a big hatbox
in the junk by Jenny's house.
"I can put my big red hat in this,"
she said.

Jenny saw a doll bed in the junk
by one house. She put her doll
in the bed. "It's just right,"
she said.

So Jenny asked for the doll bed.

By this time everyone was looking
at the junk up the street and the
junk down the street.

A man picked up a radio.
"Do you call this junk?" he said.
"I can have this radio working
in no time." And off he went with it.

A woman took home a white
doghouse and put it in her backyard.
"I've been looking for a doghouse,"
she said. "Now I can get a dog."

One man was happy to find a window box.
"I'll paint it green," he said.
"I'll put some red flowers in it."

An old man saw an old picture
of a river. "I lived by a river
when I was a boy," he said.
And he took the picture home.

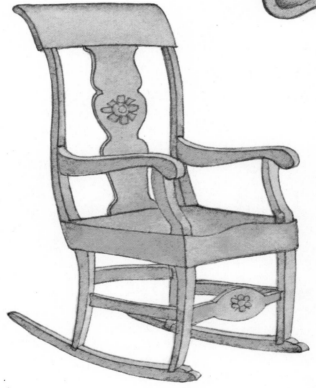

By that night there was just one thing
on Juniper Street. It was a big rocking chair.
People stopped to look at it, but everyone said,
"Too big!"

So there it was.

The next morning a big truck came
down Juniper Street.

"Oh, my," said Ben's father. "We forgot
to tell the junk man not to come!"

The truck came on down the street and stopped.
A very big man got out of the truck.
He looked up and down the street.

All he saw was the rocking chair.
He walked over and looked at it. Then
he sat down and began to rock.

At last!
A big rocking chair!

Then he put the chair on his truck,
and off he went with all the junk
on Juniper Street.

Elizabeth Levy

# The Giant Who Didn't Win

One summer day, in a place far away,
the townspeople were having an afternoon
of games. A giant who lived in a nearby castle
came by to play games, too. No one
really wanted a giant around. But no one knew
how to tell him not to come.

So the giant came, and he wanted to play
in all the games. The townspeople began
the afternoon with a game of bobbing for apples.
The giant tried, but he didn't win.
The one to win was someone from the town
of Stillwater.

The next game was to see who could paint
the best picture. The giant worked for a long time
on his picture, but he didn't win. Someone
from the town of Stillwater did. The giant said
to the man next to him, "You know, I really
thought I would win that one. I want to win
something this afternoon."

Then there was a game to see who could
sing the best. The giant made a lot of noise, but he
didn't win. Everyone said a woman from Stillwater
was the best. The giant said to anyone around,
"Who are these people from Stillwater?
I've never heard of them."

Soon the afternoon was over and the giant didn't win anything at all. The people from Stillwater were the ones to win everything.

That night the giant was sitting alone in his castle. He was feeling very mean. "I've got to find out where this town of Stillwater is," he said.

He went to his books and looked it up. "Here it is," he said. "Stillwater is near a big river. It doesn't look very far from here."

"I'm going to do something to the people
of Stillwater," said the giant. "I've got
to think of something really mean."

The giant walked from room to room,
trying to come up with an idea.

Then the giant laughed a mean laugh.
"I've got it!" he said. "I'll take a
big bag of dirt to Stillwater.
I'll dump the dirt into the river
that's near the town. The water
will come up and cover all the people and
all the town. What a good idea!"

The next day the giant got up, still feeling mean. "I feel very mean today," he said. But no one was around to hear him.

He put lots of dirt into a big bag, and he began his trip to Stillwater. Only he forgot the book that told him where Stillwater was, and he forgot to bring along something to eat.

The giant walked all day and after some time, he began to get hungry. The giant stopped a cobbler who was coming along the road. The cobbler was hungry, too, and he wanted to get home fast. He had a big bag on his back, too, but his bag had lots of old shoes in it.

The cobbler had just come from Stillwater.
The shoes were all owned by the townspeople.
He had picked up all the old shoes, and
he was taking them home to make them
look like new. Then he would take them back
to Stillwater, and everyone would pay him.

"Oh, Mr. Cobbler," said the giant. "Can you
tell me how far Stillwater is?"

The cobbler looked at the giant. The giant
was looking mean and hungry. "Why do you want
to go there?" asked the cobbler.

"I want to dump this bag of dirt
into their river," said the giant.
"The dirt will make the water
come up and cover the town.
I don't like the people in that town.
They didn't let me win anything
at their games one afternoon."

"Oh, oh," thought the cobbler.
"This will never do. If the giant
makes the water cover up Stillwater,
no one will be there to pay me
when I bring these shoes back."

The cobbler thought and thought. Then he said,
"You will never get to Stillwater today. Why, look
at me. I've just come from Stillwater. Look at
all these shoes I had to wear out just to get from there
to here." He showed the giant his bag of old shoes.

The giant sat down and cried.
"I'm hungry," he said,
"and I need my sleep.
I'll never make it
all the way to Stillwater.
I'm going back home
to my castle."

The giant dropped his bag of dirt where he had stopped.
This bag of dirt was as big as a hill. It was much
too big for anyone to move.

In time the people forgot all about the giant and
his bag of dirt. But the hill is still there,
and it is called Stonesthrow. No one knows why.
You can go there if you want to.
It's not very far from the town of Stillwater.

# The Cobbler

Crooked heels
    And scuffy toes
Are all the kinds
    Of shoes he knows.

He patches up
    The broken places,
Sews the seams
    And shines their faces.

—Eleanor Alletta Chaffee

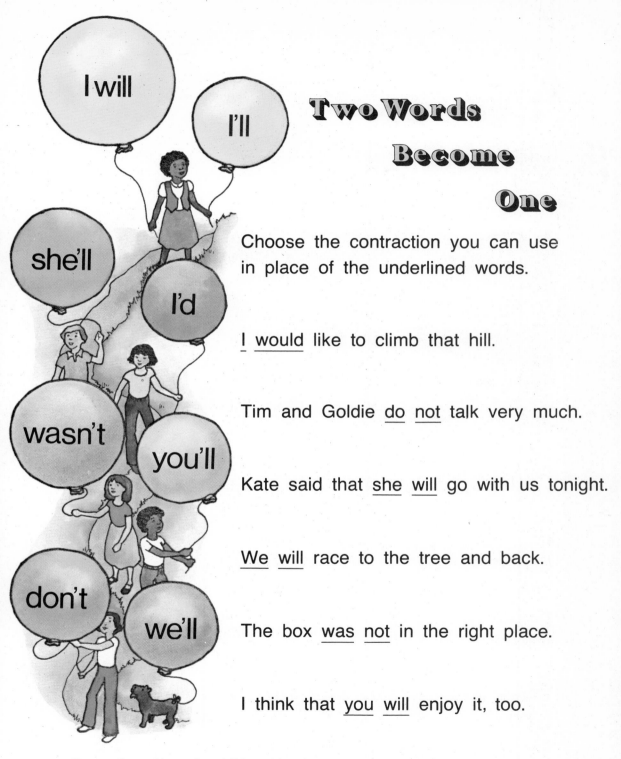

I will

I'll

she'll

I'd

wasn't

you'll

don't

we'll

# Two Words Become One

Choose the contraction you can use in place of the underlined words.

I would like to climb that hill.

Tim and Goldie do not talk very much.

Kate said that she will go with us tonight.

We will race to the tree and back.

The box was not in the right place.

I think that you will enjoy it, too.

# NO SWIMMING

George McCue

Jill, Ellen, Bob, and Edward lived near a lake.
They were good friends. And they thought
they were lucky to live so near the water.
They could go for a swim every day.

A man named Mr. Brown lived near the lake,
too. Sometimes Mr. Brown went swimming
with the children.

One day the children went to Mr. Brown's house.
They asked him to go for a swim with them.
Mr. Brown said, "We can't go for a swim.
We may never swim in the lake again."

"Why not?" asked Edward.

"Because the lake is polluted," said Mr. Brown. "There's a new sign at the lake. It was just put up today. It says:

"If we go into the water, we may get sick."

"What is making the lake polluted?" asked Jill.

"It could be a lot of things," said Mr. Brown. "Let's go down to the lake and look at it."

Mr. Brown and the children went to the lake.
They looked into the water. It wasn't clean.
They walked around the lake. And they saw
why it wasn't clean.

"Look at that garbage in the water,"
said Jill. "That's what's polluting the lake."

They walked on. Edward saw oil on the water.
"Look at that oil," said Edward. "That oil
pollutes the water, too. It comes from boats
on the lake."

"Come here," said Ellen. "Take a look
at this. Here are tires in the lake!"

"Why would people throw tires into a lake?"
asked Bob.

"They just don't stop to think,"
said Mr. Brown. "But they are not the only ones
who pollute the lake. The people who own
that factory pollute the water, too."

Bob looked at Mr. Brown. "What can we do?
How can we stop the pollution?" he asked.

"Can we make the lake clean?" asked Ellen.
"Can we ever swim in it again?"

"We can try to clean it," said Mr. Brown.
"But what good will that do? If people
pollute the lake, we can't swim in it.
The pollution must stop."

"I wish people could see what they're doing
to the lake," said Edward. "They would stop
polluting it then. I know they would."

"I know what we can do," said Mr. Brown.
"My friend Mrs. Gomez takes pictures.
Mrs. Gomez works for the newspaper. We can ask her
to take pictures of the lake. She could put
them in the newspaper. Then people would know
about the lake. They would see how they
have polluted it. They may want to help
clean it. I think Mrs. Gomez will help us."

The next day Mr. Brown went to see
Mrs. Gomez. The children went with him.
They told Mrs. Gomez about the lake.
They asked for her help. Then they took her
to see the lake. Mrs. Gomez took pictures
of the garbage. She took pictures of the oil.
She took pictures of the tires.
And she took pictures of the factory.

That night the pictures were in the newspapers.
People saw them. They talked of the pollution.
They talked of ways to clean it up.

One day people met at the lake. They came to clean it up. They cleaned out the garbage. Then they cleaned out the tires. They set up big cans. Then they put signs on the cans. The signs read, "Throw Your Garbage Here."

Some of the people had boats. They saw how their boats polluted the lake. They talked of ways to stop the oil pollution.

People from the factory were there. They came to help clean up the lake. And they looked for ways to stop polluting it.

All the people helped. They knew it would take a long time to get the lake clean. But they did not give up. They worked at it. Then one day the "No Swimming" sign came down.

Jill, Ellen, Bob, and Edward saw it come down. They were happy. They had helped the people find out about the lake. They had helped clean up the pollution. Now they could swim in the lake.

# Quiet on Account of Dinosaur

Jane Thayer

What Mary Ann liked best was finding out about dinosaurs. She had read about dinosaurs. She had pictures of them. And she had a toy dinosaur. "If I could just find one live dinosaur!" she said.

Mary Ann lived near a mountain. Whenever she climbed the mountain, she looked for dinosaurs. She was going by a cave one day when she saw something. It looked like a dinosaur's tail.

She took hold of the tail. She pulled.
Then she pulled again. A big dinosaur came out,
covering his eyes. He didn't like the sunlight.
He had been sleeping for a long time.
He was the last dinosaur in the world.
"I have found a dinosaur!" said Mary Ann.

She wanted to take him home. The dinosaur
was happy to be going some place. They went
down the mountain.

An airplane went by with a big noise.
The dinosaur looked up. He jumped. He shook.
Mary Ann told him it was only an airplane.
He still shook, but he walked along.

They came to a big road. They were
about to cross the road when a truck came by.
The dinosaur looked up. Again he jumped
and shook. He was afraid. Mary Ann told him
it was only a truck. He was still afraid.
But on he walked. Mary Ann was a little worried
about him.

They came to Mary Ann's house. Mary Ann's
mother looked at the dinosaur. She said,
"Mary Ann, you know I don't want you to bring
animals home!"

"Can't I keep him for a pet?" asked Mary Ann.

"No," said her mother. "What would we do
with him when we go away?"

"Then I'll take him to school," said Mary Ann.
She knew the children would love
to have a dinosaur for a pet. Miss Tuft
liked animals, too. Next day Mary Ann took him
to school.

She went in to tell the children she
had found a dinosaur. "Where is he?" they cried.
"He's out there," said Mary Ann.

The children went out to see the dinosaur.
"He's not afraid of us," they cried. "May we
feed him?"

"Yes," said Miss Tuft. "You may feed him.
You may never see a dinosaur again."

"What's his name?" cried the children.

Mary Ann looked at the dinosaur. She thought
for a time. "His name is Dandy," she said.

The children liked feeding Dandy. He ate
everything they gave him. He liked
the cookies best.

"May we keep him for a pet, Miss Tuft?"
Mary Ann asked.

"Yes," said Miss Tuft. "You may keep him
for a pet."

The children put Dandy in a quiet place.
They took care of him. He was happy.
And Mary Ann was happy. She had a pet dinosaur.

But then someone put the news about Dandy
in the newspaper. People began to come
from far away to see him. They came in cars.
They came in trucks. They came in airplanes.

117

Mary Ann and her friends wanted people
to come and see Dandy. The only bad thing was
there was a lot of noise around the school
now from cars and trains and airplanes.

Then Mary Ann saw that Dandy was not happy.
She saw that he covered his head and shook.

More and more people came. Now Dandy
covered his head and shook all the time.
Mary Ann was worried. "What can be wrong
with Dandy?" she thought.

Mary Ann called a famous scientist. His name
was Dr. St. George. He said he would come
right over. Mary Ann was not worried now.
Dr. St. George would find out what was wrong
with Dandy.

Dr. St. George came. He looked at
Dandy's eyes. He put his hand on Dandy's head.
"Maybe he has something," he said.

Just then a man came by in a car that made
a lot of noise. He was coming to see
Dandy the dinosaur. Dandy looked up. Then
he jumped and began to run away.

"Maybe he's afraid of people," Dr. St. George
said, bringing him back.

"No, he's not afraid of people," said
Mary Ann. "He wasn't afraid of my friends."

120

"I'll look after him for a few days," said
the famous Dr. St. George. "Where can we put
him so he won't run away?" The only place
they could think of was in the gym. Mary Ann
and Dr. St. George pulled Dandy into the gym.

When he got into the gym, Dandy put
his head up. He looked around. He stopped
jumping. "I think I know what was wrong,"
cried Mary Ann.

Just then, in the next room, the school band
began to play. The band made a lot of noise.
The noise grew and grew.

Dandy the dinosaur looked up. He jumped
and he shook.

"Stop the band!" cried Dr. St. George.
Mary Ann went out and asked the band to stop
playing. They stopped. Dandy quieted down.
Dr. St. George looked at Mary Ann.
She looked back.

"It's the noise," said Dr. St. George.
"Dandy has never heard a band before."

"Or airplanes or trucks or cars that make
a lot of noise," Mary Ann said.

"Back in his day," Dr. St. George said, "there wasn't much noise. All he ever heard was the wind and the water. And maybe some other dinosaurs talking."

"I know," said Mary Ann.

"What will we do now?" asked Dr. St. George.

"I know!" said Mary Ann. She told the other children about Dandy. She said he was afraid of only one thing—a big noise.

So the children made a sign. They put it up near the school. It said:

QUIET!
On Account of
Dinosaur

Then the school became quiet again. The people saw the sign. They put their cars in a lot far away. They came up to the dinosaur quietly.

Dandy was happy to see them. And Mary Ann was happy, too. Now she had dinosaur books and pictures and Dandy the dinosaur, too.

And when Mary Ann grew up, what do you think she did? She became a famous scientist like Dr. St. George. She became a famous scientist because she knew so much about dinosaurs.

# Birthday Gift

I know that I could have a fish
A hamster or a rabbit.
A kitten or a puppy dog
Could be a pleasant habit.
The only pet I really want
Is just a smallish dragon
To follow me about the yard
And pull me in my wagon
And toast marshmallows with his nose
And snortle very gently
And give off little sparks at night
And curl up quite contently.

124                                    —Margaret Hillert

# FINDING OUT ABOUT DINOSAURS

Long, long ago, there were no people in the world. But there were animals. One of these animals was the dinosaur. Some dinosaurs were the biggest animals that ever walked in the world. One was taller than a house of three floors. But some were as small as cats.

Some dinosaurs ate meat. These were fighters
and killed other dinosaurs. Other dinosaurs
ate plants. These were not fighters
and did not eat other dinosaurs.

Tyrannosaurus was one of the dinosaurs
that ate meat. It was a fighter. Tyrannosaurus
was about 50 feet long and 20 feet tall.
It walked on two big legs. The arms
of Tyrannosaurus were small. But it could hold
and kill other animals with its arms.
Tyrannosaurus killed other animals so that
it could live.

Brontosaurus was one of the dinosaurs that ate plants. It was about 70 feet long and 15 feet tall. Brontosaurus had a long tail and a small head. It walked on four legs. Brontosaurus lived in or near water a good part of its life. There it could find the plants it liked to eat.

Another dinosaur that ate plants was Corythosaurus. It was about 20 feet long. Corythosaurus could swim. Its feet and tail were made to help it swim.

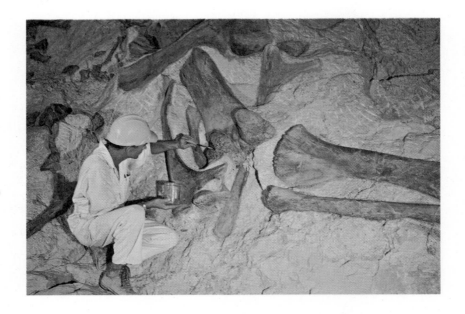

At one time dinosaurs lived in all parts
of the world. There are no dinosaurs today.
They died out long ago.

No one really knows why the dinosaurs
died out. When the dinosaurs died out,
other animals died out, too. A very big change
took place in the world. We don't know
what it was. Maybe it became colder.
The animals could not live with the change
and they died.

We know about dinosaurs today only because
their bones have been found. Their bones
have been found in all parts of the world.
They have been found in very old rocks.

People have found dinosaur bones
in this country. They have found them
in Montana and Wyoming. They have found them
in New Jersey, Pennsylvania, and New Mexico.
    People have put the bones together to make
tall skeletons. Putting a skeleton together
can take a long time. These skeletons help us
know what dinosaurs looked like long ago.

# Learning From Others

Who helps you learn? People! These people all work in the *education services*.

This woman is a *classroom teacher.* She is teaching children to read. She also teaches other subjects such as mathematics, social studies, and science. And that's a lot of teaching!

A *librarian* is also a teacher. A librarian teaches you how to use the library. This librarian is helping children choose good books to read.

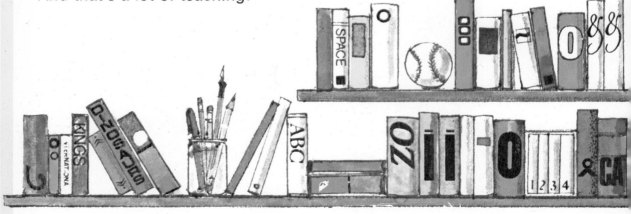

Do you know what special kind of teacher this woman is? She is an *arts and crafts teacher.* She is teaching the girl how to use a potter's wheel. The girl will use the wheel to make pots and bowls.

This man is another special kind of teacher. He is a *museum teacher.* He works at the American Museum of Natural History in New York City. What do you think he is teaching the boy?

Would you like to be a teacher when you grow up? What kind of teacher would you like to be?

# 3

# FOUR SCARY THINGS

## Giraffe! Giraffe!

Giraffe! Giraffe!
What kicky, sticky legs you've got.
What a long neck you've got. It looks like
a stick of fire.
You have dots blue, yellow, and orange.
You look like you are burning.
　　Giraffe! Giraffe!
What kicky sticky legs you've got.

—Hipolito Rivera, Age 11

# MARVIN'S

There's a big round thing on my street. I asked my mother, "What's that?"

"It's a manhole cover, Marvin," she said.

"What's a manhole cover?" I asked.

"It's something that covers up a manhole," she told me.

"But what's a manhole for?"

She told me that there are pipes and things under the street. If a man has to work on them, he goes down a special hole to get to the pipes. The hole he goes down is a manhole.

# MANHOLE

Winifred Rosen

But I didn't think that was right. I thought mother
just wanted me to stay out of that hole.
She knew I had to find out what
was down there. Maybe she thought
I'd fall into the manhole
if I took off the cover.

Maybe she thought I'd go
down that hole and never
come back. Some mothers are
like that. They think
you might never come
home from places.

But I had to know what was
down there. I had to know what
was under that manhole cover.

I thought there was a scary thing down there.
One day I went quietly over to the manhole.
I didn't want the scary thing to hear me.
I waited there for a long time. I didn't hear
it make any noise. But that didn't mean much.

I thought about that manhole a lot. Some days
I would pick up my baseball bat. I'd hit
the manhole cover. Then I'd run away fast.
The scary thing never tried to get me.
But that didn't mean it wouldn't try.

What the scary thing liked was bread.
Before I went to bed, I'd put some bread next
to the manhole. It was gone in the morning.
So I knew the scary thing liked it.

One time when I sat near the manhole, I heard
a noise. I thought, "Oh, oh! The scary thing
has prisoners trapped down there."

That night I put lots of bread near the manhole.
This time I said, "Give some of this bread
to your prisoners."

I didn't know if it would give the prisoners
the bread. So I thought I'd stay there.
If I heard a cry from the prisoners, I'd take
my baseball bat. I'd hit the monster right on
the manhole cover. That would teach it.

One day I went over to the cover. I called,
"Why don't you come out. Come and play baseball."

The scary thing didn't say a thing. I didn't
like that. So I hit the manhole cover. I hit it
with my baseball bat. I hit it again and again.
But it didn't do any good. The scary thing
still didn't come out. So I went home.

One morning I came by the manhole.
The cover was not on it.

"The scary thing ran away," I thought.
"Now where can it be?"

So I looked under the cars. I looked
in doorways. I looked around garbage cans.
I could not find that scary thing.

Then I thought, "Maybe it went back
into its hole."

I looked into the manhole. Was it dark!
Then I saw a ladder. It went right down
into the manhole. I began to climb
down the ladder.

It got darker and darker.

Then I could feel something.

It was not the ladder.

It moved!

139

141

It was a man.

"What are you doing in a manhole?" he asked.
"There isn't anything down here but some pipes."

"Do you work on the pipes?" I asked.

"Yes," he said. "Now run along
and play baseball."

The next day I saw a funny-looking thing
on our street. It looked like a cage.

I asked my mother, "What's that cage for?"

She said, "That's no cage, Marvin.
That's just where the water goes down.
It goes under the street."

But I knew that wasn't right.

A cage is a cage.

# Pretending

I have quite a handy habit.
When I hurry, I'm a rabbit.

When I'm buying chops and stew,
I'm a tiger—hungry, too!

When I meet a friendly horse,
I'm another horse, of course.

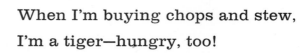

If you run and try to catch me,
I will vanish in the air.
And before you finish blinking,
I'm a most surprising bear.

So, if when you go out walking,
There's a fox behind a tree,
Don't be afraid and call for aid,
It's really only me.

—*Alice and Martin Provensen*

Elizabeth Levy

# Something Strange at the Toy Store

# The Green Rock

Betty Rubin looked around the toy store.
She waited. And she waited some more.
She didn't have much time. Today was
her brother Lou's birthday. She had to get
something right away.

Betty knew what she wanted. Lou liked
to collect rocks. And Betty saw one
that would be just right.

But Betty had to wait. She had to wait
for Mr. Konivi, who owned the toy store.
A policeman was in the store. And he
was talking with Mr. Konivi.

As Betty waited, she thought. She thought
about the policeman. What could he be doing
there? "Something strange is going on,"
she said quietly.

Then Betty heard the policeman say
that something was missing. Betty didn't hear
what it was. What could it be? Just then
Mr. Konivi came over to her.

147

"Hello, Betty," he said. "What can I do for you?" Mr. Konivi tried to smile.

"It's Lou's birthday party today," Betty said. "Lou likes to collect rocks. I want to give him that small, green one."

Mr. Konivi reached for the rock. He looked at it. "I don't know how much this one is," he said. "Mr. Burt forgot to put a tag on it. And I can't look it up right now."

Mr. Burt worked for Mr. Konivi. He took the toys out of the boxes. He also took care of the bills for the toys. These bills would tell him how much the toys were. Then he put tags on the toys.

Mr. Konivi put the rock in a small box. He gave the box to Betty. "You can pay me when you come in again," he said.

"Thank you," said Betty. She smiled at Mr. Konivi, but she was thinking about Mr. Burt.

"Why did he forget to tag this rock?" she thought. "Something strange is going on."

Mr. Konivi went back to the policeman. They began talking again. Betty couldn't hear what they were saying. So she went home.

When Betty got home, Lou's friends were
there. They had come to see Lou on his birthday.
They had come with new toys for him.
They were all smiles. And Lou was all smiles,
too. He had lots of new toys for his birthday.

Betty gave Lou the rock. She knew
that he liked it from the way he smiled.
When no one was looking, he quietly told Betty
that he liked the green rock best.

For a time everyone played in the house.
Then they went into the backyard to play.
Some of them climbed into the treehouse.

Lou sat near the door of the treehouse.
Betty was the last one to climb the ladder.
She saw her mother come out of the house.
With her was Mr. Burt from the toy store.

"Mr. Burt is coming to tell me how much
the rock is," Betty thought.

"Betty," called Mrs. Rubin. "Please
come down. Mr. Burt is here. He would like
to talk with you. He says it's about the rock
you gave to Lou."

Betty came down the ladder. "What is it?"
Betty asked Mr. Burt.

The man looked upset. He looked more upset
than Mr. Konivi had that morning.

"Please give the jade back," he said.
"I need it."

"The what?" asked Betty.

"The green rock you got in the store," said
Mr. Burt. "It's jade. It's worth a lot.
And I need it."

"Why do I have to give it back?" asked Betty.

"Mr. Konivi should not have let it go,"
said Mr. Burt. "A man wants that jade.
He came into the toy store the other day.
He saw the jade.

"I told him what it was worth. He asked me to save it for him. That's why I took off the tag. Mr. Konivi didn't know. So he let you have it. Now we need it back."

"Lou collects rocks. I gave the jade to him for his birthday," Betty said. "I can't ask for it back."

Mr. Burt looked more and more upset. "I have a rock that is just as beautiful. It's right here. You can have it if you give me the jade."

"Why don't you give that one to the man?" asked Betty.

"I can't," Mr. Burt said.

"I think you should give the jade back, Betty," said Mrs. Rubin. "I think Lou will say it's all right." She looked up at Lou.

Again Betty thought something strange was going on. But she could do nothing about it. She began to climb the ladder. She asked Lou for the rock.

Lou looked down at the treehouse floor. He was looking for the rock. He had put it on the floor near the door.

"It's gone!" he said.

"It's gone!" Betty called down.

"Gone!" said Mr. Burt.

"It was here on the floor," said Lou.

"Look again," Mrs. Rubin said.

The other children looked, too. But no one could find the jade.

"We can't find it, Mother," said Betty and Lou. "It was here. But now it's gone."

"It's got to be there," said Mr. Burt. "I'm going to take a look." He made a move for the treehouse ladder.

"No, Mr. Burt," said Mrs. Rubin. "Please don't go up there. The treehouse is just for the children. The ladder may not hold you."

"The jade must be up there some place," Mr. Burt said.

"I'll tell you what," said Mrs. Rubin.
"You go back to the store. I'll help look for
the jade. If someone finds it, we'll bring
it in."

Mr. Burt wasn't very happy. But there was
nothing more he could do. Mrs. Rubin showed
him out of the yard.

The children waited for them to go. Then
they all began to talk at once.

"Where did that rock go?" asked one child.

"Did someone hide it?" asked another.

"Mr. Burt really wanted it back, didn't he?"
Betty said, "We have to find it. Let's all
look again."

They looked everywhere in the treehouse.
It was not there.

"Maybe it dropped out of the treehouse,"
Betty said. "It was so near the door."

All the children climbed down the ladder.
They began to look under the tree. But there
were green plants all around the tree. It was
a good place for a green rock to hide.

# The Trap

Then Betty thought she saw something.
It was the green rock! Right in the middle
of some green plants!

"It's good we found it after Mr. Burt
went away!"

"Why?" asked Lou.

Betty told the children about what went on
at the toy store. She told what the policeman
said to Mr. Konivi. And she told how Mr. Burt
did not put a tag on the jade.

"I think Mr. Burt made up that story,"
said Betty. "I don't think a man wants
this jade. Mr. Burt wants it. Maybe it is
very special."

"He said it was worth a lot," Lou said.

"Maybe this jade is stolen," said Betty.
"Maybe the toy store is where Mr. Burt hides stolen things."

"You could be right, Betty," said Lou.
"Let's tell Mother."

Betty and Lou ran to tell Mrs. Rubin.

Mrs. Rubin thought about Betty's story.

"I'm going to call the police," she said.

Soon, a car stopped at the Rubins' house.
A policeman got out of the car. It was
the policeman who had been in the toy store.
Betty ran to open the door for him.
And she told her story all over again.

The policeman looked at Betty. "I think you're right," he said. "I went to the store this morning to talk to Mr. Konivi. The police have been looking for some stolen jade. We've looked all over for it. Mr. Konivi has rocks in his store. We thought he might know something about it."

"Did Mr. Konivi know anything about it?" asked Betty.

"No," said the policeman. "But he did tell me about the missing tag. We looked at the bills for the rocks. There was no bill for the jade. We knew then that Mr. Burt was up to something."

"Mr. Burt really wants that jade," said Betty. "I think he'll come back for it. He may try tonight."

"He just might," said the policeman. "And maybe we can trap him."

"One way," said Betty, "would be to put the jade back up in the treehouse. Mr. Burt will want to look there for it."

"It's worth trying," the policeman said.
"As soon as it gets dark, I'll come back
with my men. I'll hide in your treehouse.
And my men will hide nearby. If Mr. Burt
comes for the jade, we will trap him."

That night the Rubins stayed indoors. They
waited. Mr. Konivi came to sit with them.

The TV was on, but Betty was not looking
at it. She would have liked to be outdoors.
She wanted to know what was going on.
She wanted to see if the trap would work.

After a long time the policeman came
to the door. Other policemen were putting
Mr. Burt into the police car. The Rubins
heard the story.

Mr. Burt had come back. He climbed
the ladder and went into the treehouse.
He found the jade on the treehouse floor.
And he found a policeman's hand on him.

"What's going on? Let me go! Let me go!"
Mr. Burt had said. At first he thought
it was one of the children. But then
the policeman took the jade from his hand.

Mr. Burt could hear the other men.
He could not get away. He came down the ladder
quietly.

Mr. Konivi left the Rubins' house
with the policeman. He had to talk to the police
about Mr. Burt. Mr. Konivi was happy that Betty
had helped him. He thanked her over and over
again.

The story was in the newspaper the next day. With the story was a picture. It was of Betty and Lou.

Mrs. Rubin and Mr. Konivi were there, too. Betty was the one in the middle. But you knew that, didn't you?

# Conserving Our Resources

People everywhere need air and water and sunshine. They need land. They need the things that come from the land. They need animals. And, of course, they need other people. Our country is very rich in all of these natural resources. The people in these photographs help us to save, or conserve, those resources.

Do you like outdoor life? If so, you might like to be a *forest ranger*, like this man. Forest rangers protect our forests from fire, insects, and disease. They also help care for our national parks and wildlife sanctuaries.

This man is an *environmental chemist.* His job is to help keep our environment free of pollution. Here he is testing for water pollution.

Do you know where paper comes from? From trees! This woman is a *forester*. She works for a paper company. Here she is measuring a tree. She wants to find out how fast the tree is growing. When she knows this, she can tell how much wood it will yield. Then people will be able to plan just how many trees they need to cut down. They will also be able to plan how many new trees to plant.

This woman is taking samples of the soil. She is a *soil scientist*. She is looking for ways to help farmers make the best possible use of their land.

Who else works to help us conserve our natural resources? How can you help?

165

TALKING PICTURES

**Oral Communication.** Discuss the "problem situation" in each frame. Then have children role play possible solutions to each problem.

# Tammy Camps in the Rocky Mountains

Mary Elizabeth Baker

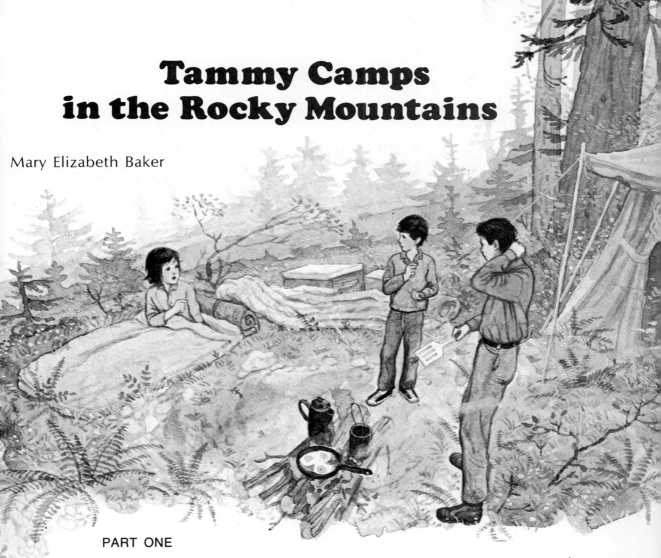

PART ONE

## Long's Peak

Tammy sat up. She was still in her sleeping bag. She looked at her father and her brother, Terry. "Why are you up already?" she asked.

"Already!" said Daddy. "Did you forget? It's the day we climb Long's Peak. And we have to be down here again before the noonday storm."

Tammy got up and got ready to go. Daddy put all the things they would need for the trip into the pack.

"Don't forget your camera, Tammy," said Terry. "You can get some good pictures at Long's Peak."

Tammy had a new camera. She took a lot of pictures. She took the pictures to show her friend Ann. Ann did not know what it was like to set up a camp.

"Ann doesn't think camping is fun," said Tammy. "But she will when she sees my pictures."

Daddy, Terry, and Tammy went up the trail.

"Stop, you two," Tammy said. "I want to take a picture of you on the trail. Daddy, get behind Terry. Then the pack will show."

When they got to a small stream, Tammy
made them stop again. "Terry, you pick
some mountain flowers. Daddy, you sit
near the stream," she said.

Daddy and Terry laughed. But they did
as Tammy asked. Then they climbed
along the stream to the part of the mountain
where there were no more trees. And Tammy
stopped again.

"Daddy, get on that big rock. Then
turn and look at the peak," said Tammy.
Tammy walked all around him. At last she took
the picture.

"Now can we go?" Terry asked.

"Not yet," said Tammy. "Get up on the rock, and I'll take a picture of you."

"You have a picture of the peak already," said Terry.

"But I want one from the other side," said Tammy. "I want Ann to see how far up the mountain we went."

"All right," Terry said. "But if we don't get going, we won't make it to Long's Peak before the storm."

"This is the last one, Tammy," Daddy said.
Tammy took the picture. Then Daddy and Terry
turned up the trail. Tammy tried to stay
with them. But soon she was far behind them.

Tammy heard a noise behind her. She turned
to see what it was. There was a squirrel.
It was looking at her from behind some rocks.
As quietly as she could, she got her camera.
She was all set to take the picture.

"Tammy, come up here," called Terry.

The squirrel ran away. Tammy walked
to where Terry was waiting on the trail.

"We don't have time for pictures," Terry
said. "We want to miss the storm."

# Chasm Lake

Daddy looked at the sun. "I don't think
we can get all the way to the top. Not
before noon," he said. "What do you want to do?"

"Let's go on," said Terry. "Let's see
how far we can get."

"That's not a good idea," said Daddy.
"Don't forget the storm."

"I guess that wouldn't be so good,"
Terry said. He turned to his sister.
"You and your camera!"

"Let's think of lunch," said Daddy.
"Where can we go for lunch?"

"If we can't go to Long's Peak, let's go
to Chasm Lake," said Tammy. "Wouldn't that be
a good place for lunch? It's just minutes away."

"I think it would," said Daddy.

Along the way they saw a waterfall. It was
beautiful. Tammy stopped to look at it.

"I wish I could get a picture of that,"
said Tammy. "But I can't get one from here."

"There will be other pictures you can get,"
Daddy said. He started down the trail. Tammy
and Terry came behind him.

"What's that little house?" Tammy asked.

"It's a place to stay if you're on the mountain in a storm," Daddy said.

"Can we go in it?" asked Tammy.

"In a few minutes," Daddy said. "Let's go and look at Chasm Lake first." Daddy began to climb the rocks behind the little house. Tammy and Terry went ahead of him. They wanted to see who could get to the top first.

"Oh, it's beautiful!" said Tammy as she looked over the side of a big rock and saw Chasm Lake for the first time. She got out her camera and took a picture.

"Come on down here," Terry called. "I'll take a picture of you with the lake behind you."

Tammy climbed down off the rock and walked over to the lake.

"I can't get you there," Terry said. "Back up."

Tammy started to back up, hit her foot on a rock, and sat down in the water.

"Oh, Terry, help! It's cold!" she cried. "Why didn't you tell me I was so near the water?"

Terry helped Tammy up. He handed her
the camera. "That's a good picture,"
he laughed.

"Did you take one of me in the water?"
asked Tammy. "You won't take a picture
with my camera again!"

"Let's get back to the house," said Daddy.
"Tammy can dry off there. And we can have
lunch there, too."

They went back to the little house. Tammy
took a cover off the bed. She put it
around her. "It's cold in here," she said.
"I'm going out in the sun to dry off."

They sat in the sun to eat their lunch.
Then they saw a big cloud. Soon the sky
began to get dark. They could not see
the top of the mountain.

"Here comes the noonday storm," said Daddy.
"Let's get back into the house."

Just as they got inside, the rain started.
They all looked out at the storm. It was
only a few minutes before the rain stopped.
Then the sun came out again.

"Time to go," said Daddy.

Tammy put the cover back on the bed.
They started along the trail.

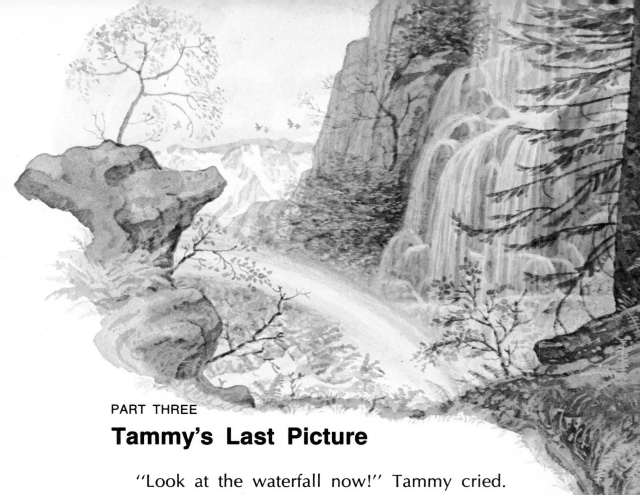

PART THREE

# Tammy's Last Picture

"Look at the waterfall now!" Tammy cried. "There's a rainbow! I want to get a picture of that."

Tammy ran up the trail. She came to a place where she could take the picture. She sat down on the side of the trail. Then she slid part way down the mountain. Her feet came to rest on a big rock. From there she took the picture.

"Tammy, come back here," Daddy called.

"Just one more picture," Tammy said. "I want to get the rainbow again."

Tammy moved a little. She wanted to get a good picture of the rainbow. The rock under her feet started to move. It slid down the mountain. Behind it slid Tammy, feet first.

"Daddy, help!" Tammy cried. She tried to stop her fall. She took hold of some small plants. But the plants came up in her hands. At last her feet found another rock. Tammy came to a stop.

Tammy was afraid. She called out, "Daddy! Daddy! Help me!"

"How will we get her up?" Terry asked.
"There's no telling how long that rock she's on
will stay in place."

"Get the rope from my pack," Daddy said.
Then he looked down at Tammy. "It's all right,
Tammy. We'll get you. Hold on. I'm going
to throw a rope down. We'll pull you up.
Here it comes, Tammy," said Daddy.

The rope fell down the mountain,
about a foot away from Tammy.

"I see it," Tammy called.
She got the rope and turned away
from the mountain.

"What are you doing?" Daddy cried.

"I want to take that picture," Tammy said.

"Look out, Tammy!" Daddy called. "The rock is moving!"

Just as the rock slid, Tammy took the picture. The big rock went faster and faster. Down the mountain it went. Soon they couldn't see it. But Tammy was holding onto the rope.

"We'll get you up," Daddy said. "Just hold on tight a few minutes more."

They started to pull Tammy up. They pulled her a little at a time. Dirt and rocks slid out from under her. But at last they got Tammy back to the top of the mountain.

"It's all right," Daddy said. "You don't have to be afraid now. We pulled you up. Just rest a few minutes."

Tammy rested. Then she cried, "My camera! Is it all right?"

Terry and Daddy looked at the camera. They smiled. "Your camera is safe," Daddy said. "Now let's get back on the trail."

Daddy, Terry, and Tammy started down the trail. Once, Tammy stopped to take a picture. But Daddy took the camera out of her hands.

"No more pictures on this trip, Tammy," he said. "If Ann wants to know more about the Rocky Mountains, you can tell her."

# Other Words Can Help!

What other words in each sentence below
help you know the meaning of the underlined word?
Which picture fits the sentence?

The apple is <u>bobbing</u>
up and down in the water.

Shep <u>collects</u> toy trains
and likes to keep them
on a special table.

I became <u>worried</u> when
my cat was gone so long.

<u>Squirrels</u> are small animals
that like to live and play
in trees.

**Context Clues.** Often we can find the meaning of a word from the other words
around it. Have the children discuss what other words in each sentence help them
to understand the underlined word. Then let them choose the picture that shows
what the sentence means.

Joan Lexau

# The Potter and the Tiger

PART ONE

## The Potter

Once there was a potter. One night,
the potter was looking for his burro.
The night was dark. And it was raining.
"Come, my dear burro," the potter called.
"Where are you, good burro?"
To himself he said, "Such a night to be out!
Wait until I get my hands on that burro.
It won't walk off again!"

The potter could not see well in the rain.
He did not know he was near a tiger.
When the tiger moved, the potter jumped on it.
He hit it. Then he gave it a kick.

"You must not run away again on such a night,"
said the potter. "Now come home, burro!"

The tiger was never so surprised. It let
the potter ride home on its back.

In the morning the potter's wife talked to him.
"What did you ride home last night?" she said.

"The burro," said the potter. "Why do you ask?"

"Look out there," said his wife.

The potter was surprised to see the tiger.
"Oh dear, dear, dear," he said. "That tiger
could kill a person! What did he do to me?"

His wife looked him over. "I think
you're all right," she said.

Soon people saw the tiger. They asked why
it was by the potter's house. Then the story
got around. From near and far, people came.
They had to hear the story from the potter.

The potter told his story. But he would not tell
how he thought the tiger was his burro.
And he would end with, "It was nothing.
Nothing at all."

"Nothing! That big tiger! Once he made us
afraid to go out at night," a man cried.
"Now we're not afraid. The king should hear
of this. We must tell the king."

The people went to the king. They told him
of the potter's ride on the tiger. The king
was surprised. He had never heard of such a man.
Here was a man who could bring back a tiger
with nothing but his two hands. The king
did not wait to hear more. He said that he
must see this man for himself.

At once the men took the king
to the potter's house.

The potter gave the tiger to the king.
The king liked the potter. He gave the potter
some land and a new house.

Then the king was gone. The potter said
to himself, "Well, that's over. I'll not ride
a thing but a burro again." But the potter
did not know what was in store for him.
And that was just as well.

PART TWO

# The Brave Little Potter

One day the king heard some news. A big army
was on its way to take over his castle.
The army was from a far off country.

The king called in his top men at once.
The men were upset. They said, "Our army
is too small. We can't fight such a big army.
We will have to give up."

"Not without a fight," said the king.
"Is there no brave man to lead my army?"

"There is," cried one of the men. "The man who got the tiger with nothing but his two hands. He is the brave man to lead our army."

"Bring the potter to me," said the king.

The potter came to the king. He was surprised to hear that he must lead the king's army.

"Who, me?" asked the potter.

"You, my brave man," said the king.

Does a brave man say "no" to the king? The potter was not that brave. "Does the enemy have a big army?" he asked.

"I don't know," said the king.

"I'll find out," said the potter. "I'll go out alone to see how big their army is."

The potter went home. "Wife," he said.
"I must ride out to look at the enemy's army.
We still don't have a burro. Will you find me
a horse? Now I have never been on a horse.
So get me a small one. I mean a pony.
I mean a small pony."

"I'm a potter," he thought. "I'm not a man
to lead an army."

He waited for his wife to say, "You must not go."
But she did not say a thing. She went out
and got a pony for him.

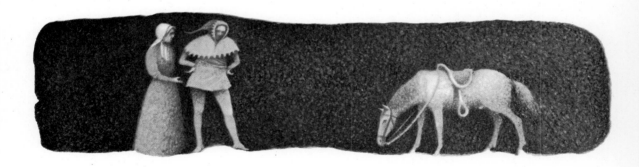

The potter looked at the pony. "Couldn't you find
a smaller one than that?" he asked.

"There is no smaller pony," said his wife.

Just then a man came from the king. With him
was a charger.

"The king wants you to ride this horse,"
the man said.

"Oh dear, dear, dear," said the potter.
"Well, I can't ride the pony when the king wants
me to ride this horse." He waited for his wife
to say he could ride the pony after all.

"This charger will go much faster
than that little pony," she said.

"I know, I know," said the potter. He looked
at the charger and said he would not go just yet.
He would go at night. "After all, I want to see
the enemy, but I don't want them to see me,"
he said.

## PART THREE

# The Potter Rides Again

Soon it was dark. The potter's wife told him it was time to go.

"Not yet," the potter said. "Let it get darker."

"It won't get any darker than this," said his wife. And she went to get the charger.

Now the potter had never been on a horse. But he got on the charger. Only he was looking one way. And the horse was looking the other way.

"This is no good," said the potter. "I must see where I'm going." He jumped off and got on the right way.

"Quick," he said to his wife. "Put a rope around me so I won't fall off this horse."

His wife did as she was told. He waited for her to say he must not go. He waited for her to say if the horse did not kill him, the enemy would.

"Well," said the potter.

"Take care," said the wife.

The charger began to kick and jump, and then the potter was off.

"Didn't you hear my wife? She said
to take care," the potter said to the horse.

The charger ran on. It ran so fast
that the potter could not see where they were.
The charger ran all night.

In the morning they came to the enemy's camp.
The potter did not want to charge through it.
He did not want the enemy to kill him.

"Stop!" he called. "Stop! Stop!"
But the horse did not stop.

"Oh dear, dear, dear," said the potter.
"What will I do?"

The potter saw a small tree. He took hold of it
to stop the horse. But the charger was going
so fast that the tree came up in the potter's hands.

Some of the men in the enemy camp saw him.
"Look! Look at that man
on that big charger. He looks very mad.
See, he is picking up trees as he rides!"
said one man.

"The rest of his army must be coming
behind him. If they are all like him,
we'll be killed," another man said.

They ran to tell their king that a big army
was coming and picking up trees as they came.

"We can't fight men like that!" they said.
"Quick! Quick! Let's get out of here.
We'll be killed if we stay and fight!"

The king and his men got away as fast
as they could. Only one man stayed behind.
He was too afraid to move.

The potter fell off the horse when he got
to the enemy camp. The horse stopped, too.
It could run no more. The potter knew
that the enemy would kill him. He waited
for them to do it.

At last he looked around. He saw the man
who stayed behind. The man told the potter
that the army was gone. There would be no fight.
The man asked if he would be killed.

"No," said the potter. "I'm not going to kill you.
You may go home."

The potter couldn't wait to get back
to his house, where it was safe.
He was through riding horses, so he took
the charger and walked home.
When he got home, it was dark. His wife saw
him through the window and ran out
of the house.

"I was so afraid you would be killed,"
she said. "I didn't want you to go."

"**Now** you tell me," the potter said.

The potter called to a man, "Take this horse
to the king. Thank him for letting me ride it.
And tell him that I'll see him in the morning."

In the morning the potter went to see the king.
He set out on foot. Two men saw him.

One man said, "Look at him. All by himself
he made the enemy run. Yet he goes to the king
on foot."

"Yes," said the other man. "He could go
on that beautiful horse. But he doesn't want
to show how brave a man he is."

The king came out of the castle and thanked the potter for his brave deed. "You may have anything you want," said the king. "Just ask, and it will be yours."

"There is only one thing I want," said the potter. "Never to ride a horse again!"

# Moodpic

Listen to the roaring
wind howling like
a nighttime
tiger,
Bursting in, bowing
down trees and
shaking hairy
branches.

—Estelle Banks, Age 10

# HOW WOULD YOU FEEL?

## Wish

I know what *I* feel like;
I'd like to be *you*
And feel what *you* feel like
And do what *you* do.
I'd like to change places
For maybe a week
And look like your look-alike
And speak as you speak
And think what you're thinking
And go where you go
And feel what you're feeling
And know what you know.
I wish we could do it;
What fun it would be
If I could try *you* out
And you could try me.

—Mary Ann Hoberman

# The Treehouse

Dina Anastasio

It was the day of Lisa's birthday.
Lisa climbed the big tree in her backyard.
She knew she should not be climbing a tree.
Not in her new clothes! But Lisa did not care.
The children would soon be there for her party.
Lisa wanted to be in her treehouse then.

Lisa thought a lot about her party.
Whenever she did, she got a strange feeling.
"The party will be just horrible," she thought.
Lisa was new in town. She had just moved there.
Lisa did not know the children in town.
She did not know the ones who would be
at her party. On the first day of school,
she met them. But they were not her friends.
She did want to be friends with them.
But Lisa was shy.

Lisa did not want the party. Her mother
wanted it. Her mother wanted her to get to know
the children in town. She thought that a party
would be a good way to do that. Now Lisa
wanted to hide. Her party would be horrible!
She would hide in her treehouse.

Before long Lisa heard a car. It stopped
at her house. Three girls got out. Lisa
could see them from the tree. She could hear
her mother and father. They were talking
to the girls. Lisa's father called her.
But Lisa did not answer. Soon more children
came to the party. Lisa's father called again.
Still she didn't answer. She was too shy.

So Lisa's father went to the tree.
He picked up the telephone that he and Lisa
had made. He tapped on it three times.
Lisa picked up her telephone.

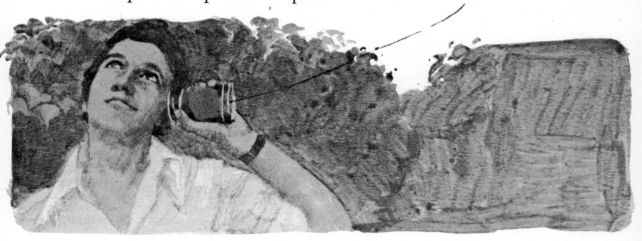

"Hello," said Lisa.

"Is this Miss Lisa Stone?" asked her father.

"Yes," said Lisa.

"Miss Stone," said her father. "Your name
has just been picked. It was picked
from a bowl filled with names. You may win
a beautiful brown kitten **if** you can answer
this question. Are you ready, Miss Stone?"

"Yes, I'm ready," Lisa laughed.

"All right, Miss Stone," said her father.
"Here is the question. What is white
on the outside and green on the inside?"

Lisa laughed. Then her father laughed, too.

"Your time is up, Miss Stone," he said. "It's too bad you can't answer the question."

"Wait," cried Lisa. "Wait! The answer is— a frog sandwich!"

"Right," her father said. He laughed. "A frog sandwich. You win. A very shy kitten is here for you. And a very happy birthday is here, too. Come and get them. Can you come down now?"

Lisa put down the telephone. She climbed down the big tree.

"A frog sandwich," laughed her father. "Really, Lisa." He gave Lisa the brown and white kitten.

Lisa looked shyly at the children. She walked over to them. She wanted to show them her kitten.

The party was not horrible. It was the best party Lisa ever had. And she had ten new friends and a kitten.

# People Need People

Look at these people at work.
They are all doing something very important.
What is it?

That's right. These people are all helping others!

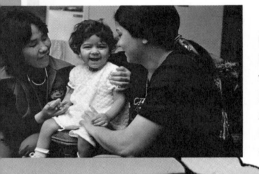

Not all nurses work in hospitals. Often nurses visit people in their homes. This *visiting nurse* is showing a mother how to take care of her baby.

This man is a *recreation worker* at a neighborhood playground. He teaches sports to children. He coaches their teams. Are there any recreation workers in your neighborhood?

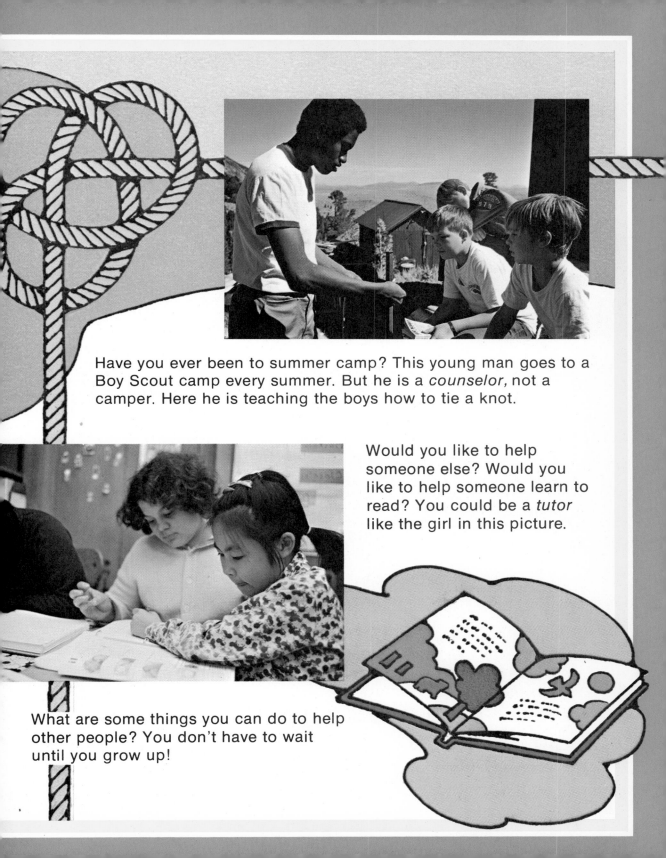

Have you ever been to summer camp? This young man goes to a Boy Scout camp every summer. But he is a *counselor*, not a camper. Here he is teaching the boys how to tie a knot.

Would you like to help someone else? Would you like to help someone learn to read? You could be a *tutor* like the girl in this picture.

What are some things you can do to help other people? You don't have to wait until you grow up!

# THE MUSIC OF MOZART

Elizabeth Levy

One day, a long time ago, the Mozart family
set out on a trip to see the king and queen.

The king and queen loved good music.
And because they were the king and queen,
they could hear the best music in the world.
Whenever they heard about people
who played music very well,
they asked them to come to the castle.

And that is why the Mozarts were
on their way to the castle. The Mozart children
were going to play for the king and queen.

Wolfgang and Nannerl Mozart were very special.
They were still children. But they could
play music as well as people
who had been playing for years and years.

Nannerl was older than Wolfgang,
and she could play very well.
But Wolfgang could play like
no other child who had ever lived.
He started playing music when he was
only three years old. And when he was five,
he wrote such beautiful music
that people still like to hear it today.

The day that the Mozart family went
to the castle, Wolfgang and Nannerl put on
their best clothes. Their mother and father
wanted them to look right and to act right
at the castle.

But when Wolfgang saw the king and queen,
he did something that surprised everyone.
He ran up to the queen and gave her a kiss.
The queen was very surprised, but she liked it.
She laughed at Wolfgang.
Then she asked everyone to sit down.

Nannerl played first, then Wolfgang.
Then the two children played together.
Their music was so beautiful, the queen began
to cry a little. The king and queen loved
the music so much, they asked the Mozarts
to come back to the castle again and again.

One time when Wolfgang was playing
for the king, the king said, "Your playing is
very beautiful with two hands. But what can
you play with one hand?"

So Wolfgang put one hand behind his back.
He showed the king how well he could play
with one hand.

Then the king said, "You play well
when you see what you are doing.
But what can you do
with your eyes covered?"

So Wolfgang's eyes were covered,
and still he played beautiful music.

When Wolfgang was alone with his father,
he told him that he didn't like doing tricks
for the king. Wolfgang said that he loved music
too much to play tricks with it.

When Wolfgang and Nannerl were at the castle,
they did not have to play music all day.
The king and queen had children of their own.
Some of them were about as old as Wolfgang
and Nannerl. The king's children and Wolfgang
and Nannerl played together all over the castle.

One day as Wolfgang was running with two
of the king's little girls, he fell.
One of the girls, Marie Antoinette, stopped
to help him up. Her sister went on walking.
Wolfgang thanked Marie Antoinette
for helping him. "When I grow up,
I will marry you," he said to her.

Marie Antoinette did not marry Wolfgang.
She was to become a queen. But she never
forgot the times she and Wolfgang played
together when they were children.

Wolfgang wrote more and more music as the
years went by. Here is a part of some music
that Wolfgang wrote when he was still only
five years old. Try to find someone to play it.

Isn't it happy music? Can you see why
the beautiful music Wolfgang Mozart wrote
years and years ago is still played today?

# Names and Pronouns

Choose the pronoun you can use
in place of the underlined words.

We      <u>Jenny</u> is playing in the backyard.

He      <u>Edward and Lou</u> were singing together.

She

They      <u>Mrs. Hunt and I</u> climbed into the helicopter.

Jim called <u>Belinda and me</u>.      him

The chipmunk jumped on <u>Teddy</u>.      her

     them

I just saw <u>Mr. Cook and Marie</u> go into the store.      us

**Pronouns.** Have the children read each sentence as it is, then with the correct pronoun in place of the underlined words.

222

# One Word – Two Meanings

I saw the <u>crane</u> fly away.
The <u>crane</u> picked up a load of dirt.
The <u>crane</u> is eating some fish.

I like to <u>watch</u> TV.
My <u>watch</u> says five o'clock.
Her <u>watch</u> does not work.

Pull up the <u>shade</u>.
We sat in the <u>shade</u>.
The bedroom <u>shade</u> is down.

I ran so fast, I had to <u>rest</u>.
You can have the <u>rest</u> of the cookies.
She will <u>rest</u> in her room.

**Multiple Meanings.** Have the first two sentences in each group read and the meanings of the underlined words discussed. Let the children choose the picture that fits each sentence. Then have the children read the third sentence and decide which meaning fits the underlined word.

# Boy, Was I Mad!

Kathryn Hitte

I was mad one day.
I mean I was really mad.
So I ran away.

I put some cookies
in my pocket
and ran out
of my house fast.

And I didn't look back.

I wouldn't look back at that house
for anything. I was so mad that day—
that day I ran away.

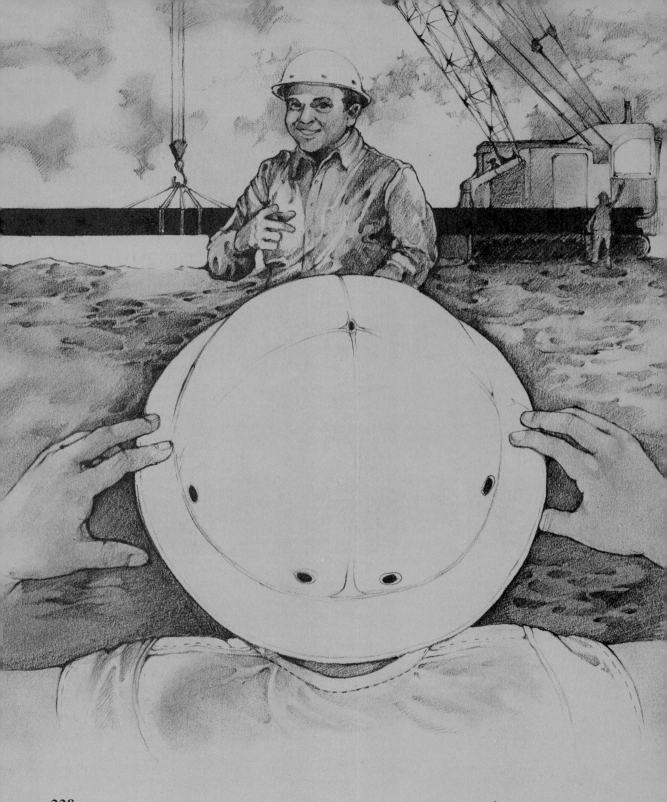

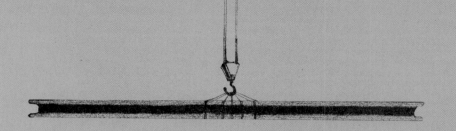

I turned the corner, and there was a crane
out over the street. Men were climbing
and working and yelling. And that crane
went up and up.

I'd like to work a thing like that crane.
I think someday I will.

"Boy!" I said. "Look at that!"

One of the workmen laughed and gave me
a hat to wear. Just like his!

It was great at that place. It was so great
I just about forgot how mad I was. But
then I remembered and went on my way.

Around the next corner I met a junk
wagon. I knew that horse and wagon. The
junk man gave me a ride—he does that a lot.

"I might have a horse of my own someday,"
I said. "I think someday I will."

It was fun on that wagon. Then I
remembered how mad I was, so I climbed
down.

I saw a dog that was after a cat, and I watched them go. Then I stopped to pet another dog, and three more old dogs came running up to me. They all began to run after me up the street. It was fun, but then I remembered I was mad.

"Look, dogs," I said. "I can't play with you now. I'm running away, see? So let me alone. Go on, go back where you came from! Go home!"

But they still walked along with me. There isn't a dog that doesn't like me. I might have lots of dogs of my own someday. I think someday I will.

Well, then I saw a lot of ants in a place
in the sidewalk. Ants are about the best
thing there is to watch.

If I hadn't been so mad, I could have stayed
there and watched the ants all day.

Around the next corner I saw Tim
and his dad and his grandma.

"We're going to the park," Tim said.
"Come along with us, Ted!" (That's me.)

I like to run and talk and horse around
in the park with Tim. I was mad, but—

"All right," I said. "I'll go."

We got to the park, and Tim's dad and
grandma sat down on a bench to talk. But
Tim and I did tricks and things like
walking on our hands.

And we climbed around on some big rocks
and watched the clouds. And we thought
about how it is that birds know how to fly.
We had a great day.

236

When I came home, there was a moon in the sky. That was funny because it was still daylight. I never saw the moon in the daytime before.

"I bet I go to the moon someday," I said. "I'm going to get to that old moon. You wait and see!"

Then just as I got to my house I thought. "I FORGOT! I'm HOME! I was going to run away. What should I do?"

Well it was time to eat, and something smelled good. Boy, did I eat! And it was a funny thing, but I just wasn't mad anymore.

When I told my mother about how I forgot
I was running away, she said, "Oh, Teddy,
I'm so happy you forgot and came back
home."

"Me, too," I said.

My mother didn't have to tell me to get
ready for bed. Boy, did it feel good, that bed.

That was some day—that day when
I ran away.

# Angry

Sometimes when the day is bad
And someone's made me very mad
Or I've been given angry stares,
I go behind the front porch stairs.

There, curled up with chin on knee,
I like to be alone with me
And listen to the people talk
And hurry by me on the walk.

There I sit without a sound,
And draw stick pictures on the ground.
If I should tire of it all,
I throw some pebbles at the wall.

After I've been there awhile
And find that I can almost smile,
I brush me off and count to ten
And try to start the day again.

—Marci Ridlon

241

Arlene Egelberg

# Please, Call Her Do-Re-Mi

Midori was a little girl who lived in Japan. She loved music. She loved to play with friends. She loved to say things in English at school. That was fun!

Best of all, Midori loved to wear her beautiful kimono. Midori did not wear it to school. She did not wear it to play outside. Her kimono was something to wear only on special days.

One day Midori and her family moved
to the United States. When it was time
to go to school, Midori felt happy.
She said, "I'm going to wear my kimono today.
It's a special day for me. It's my first day
of school in the United States."

At school all of the children looked
and looked. They had never seen a kimono.
Midori didn't know that. She thought,
"I must look funny."

When Midori said something, the class was
so quiet. Everyone wanted to hear her talk.
Midori thought, "I must talk funny."

Midori did not know all the games
that the other children played. And she
did not want to ask.

Midori said things in English very little
now. The children heard her voice only when
the class had music. Midori had a good voice.
She loved to sing. Her voice rang out
like a pretty bell.

Marvin, a boy in the class, tried to be
friendly. He hoped Midori would feel at home.
When she first came to school, Marvin helped her
to find her way around. He showed Midori
where things were in the room and outside, too.
But she never said a thing.

Then Marvin tried to make Midori laugh. Because she loved music, he called her Do-re-mi.

Midori thought about that name. It was like hers. But it was not hers. She did not like the new name. It did not make her happy.

One day there was a fire in the town. Renee, a girl in Midori's class, lived in the building that burned. Renee and her family lost everything they owned.

Midori remembered a time in Japan
when there was a fire. It was in the town
where she lived. She was sorry for Renee.

In Japan everyone in the town helped
the people who had the fire. Soon the people
felt better.

That night Midori looked at all of her things
very carefully. Midori took out an obi.
An obi is the sash on the kimono. Then
she put the obi on the floor and started
to work.

The next morning, Midori left for school.
She had a box in her hand.

In the classroom she waited. The bell rang
for lunch. Renee left the room. Midori
quickly left the box on Renee's table.

The bell rang after lunch. Renee came back.
She looked at the box in a surprised way.
There was a note on the box. It said,
"Dear Renee, I hope that this makes you feel
better!" The note was not signed.

Renee opened the box. There was a lovely
doll. It was not like any other dolls
she had ever had. But it was so pretty!
As Renee looked at her doll, she said,
"I'm so happy. When we had the fire,
I lost my doll Maria. I didn't care
about my other things. But I loved Maria
so much. Now I have a new doll to love."

Everyone was very happy for Renee.
But who had left the doll for Renee?
No one could say.
Then Marvin said, "Let's see the note."
He looked at it carefully. He walked over
to the place where the children's best papers
were. He put the note near one of the papers.

All at once Renee said, "Look at
the doll's dress! Isn't it like Midori's sash?"

"What sash?" asked one of the children.

"You remember," said Renee, "The sash
that Midori had on, the first day of school.
The red one with all the pretty flowers on it."

"You mean the obi," said Marvin. Then
he said, "But you're right. The doll's dress
is just like Midori's obi. The writing
on the note is hers, too. It's just like
her class paper."

All eyes turned to Midori.

"Midori," said Marvin, "it was *you,*
wasn't it? That was a nice thing to do!"

"Yes, it was," said the other children.

Midori watched as Marvin went on. She began
to feel happy.

"I started calling you Do-re-mi because I
hoped you'd say something. You were so quiet.
You weren't very friendly. But you really are
friendly, aren't you? Come talk with us.
Tell us about Japan."

She told the children about her life
in Japan. Her English was good. The children
were quiet. They really wanted to hear
what she had to say. Midori felt good all over!

Then Renee said, "I must have a name
for my doll."

"Why not call her Midori?" said Marvin.

"No," said Midori. "Please call her
Do-re-mi! Do-re-mi is a good name
in the United States."

Everyone laughed. "That's a good idea!"
said Renee.

# the sun

I told the Sun that I was glad,
    I'm sure I don't know why;
Somehow the pleasant way he had
    Of shining in the sky,
Just put a notion in my head
    That wouldn't it be fun
If, walking on the hill, I said
    "I'm happy" to the Sun.

—John Drinkwater

# New Words

The words listed beside the page numbers below are introduced in *People Need People*, Level 9 in HOLT BASIC READING SERIES. Italicized words can be identified from previously taught skills.

12. *Freddy*
    *boat*
    *stone*
    *another*
    dropped
13. have
    *croak*
    *Freddy's*
    *hands*
14. pocket
15. *by*
    *saying*
    Mr. Mays
16. *fishing*
    *bait*
    *drop*
    under
17. running
    *met*
    Miss Denny
    I'd
19. pond
20. *onto*
22. Christina
    Katerina
    TV
    *or*
23. *Christina's*
    tower
    castle
    Watson
    *ate*
    *locked*
    sorry
    *ten*

times
24. *kick*
    *takes*
    *clubhouse*
    *lock*
    *club*
25. *talked*
    until
    caved
26. *racing*
    *race*
    before
    *taking*
    raced
    won
    *sawed*
    *fell*
    apart
27. *dance*
    *flat*
    *coats*
    danced
28. mopped
    *let's*
29. *boats*
30. hunter
    *sun*
    *shines*
    Indian
    *tribe .*
    hunt
    *grandfather*
31. *cannot*
    *well*
    *today*

*brave*
son
*kill*
32. *fast*
    catch
    *ways*
34. *walks*
    Indians
    chief
    *chief's*
    *thing*
35. *plants*
    runs
36. *opens*
    *free*
37. healer
    *moon*
38. *thinks*
    need
    heal
39. *picks*
40. *healed*
    great
41. *Little Wolf's*
44. *wet*
    Albert
    *cloud*
    *clouds*
    *floating*
    along
    *rained*
    rain
    *schoolwork*
45. *top*
    *Albert's*

river
idea
46. *set*
    whenever
    *anyone*
    *things*
    *cows*
    *whatever*
    *life*
48. drought
    summer
    dried
    *rivers*
50. *lucky*
    farmers
    *farms*
51. harvest
    *fall*
    around
    world
    helicopter
    *bringing*
52. nothing
    *ever*
    *you'll*
54. Rumpelstiltskin
    daughter
    *king*
    *spin*
    straw
55. *cry*
    funny
    *crying*
56. give
    *man's*

58. ring
queen
59. become
child
60. became
61. guess
names
62. Mr. Appleflower
Mr. Greenpot
Mr. Crabtree
63. Mr. Birdwing
Mr. Whitecoat
Mr. Tigerbutton
64. queen's
thanked
65. Mr. Goodfish
Mr. Pennypond
cried
70. Maxie
brownstone
shades
Maxie's
living
shade
knew
71. five
sets
stairs
newspaper
hold
foot
always
closed
72. tea
teakettle
whistle
73. mail carrier
mail
74. needs
Monday
moved

asleep
you're
first
75. Tuesday
windows
76. upset
Mrs. Greenhouse
Penny Parks
77. she's
doesn't
feel
sings
79. needed
hear
80. junk
Juniper
really
backyard
Mike's
talking
Hmmm
81. Sandy's
82. mothers
Jenny's
83. clean-up
radio
doghouse
rocking
chair
84. we're
Ben's
86. table
hatbox
doll
88. call
working
91. rock
92. giant
win
townspeople
having

bobbing
Stillwater
94. feeling
mean
95. trying
bag
dirt
dump
cover
hungry
cobbler
shoes
97. owned
pay
99. hill
move
100. Stonesthrow
104. swimming
Jill
lake
Mr. Brown's
children
105. polluted
106. clean
garbage
polluting
oil
pollutes
tires
107. pollute
factory
pollution
must
108. they're
Mrs. Gomez
works
109. newspapers
110. cleaned
cans
112. account
dinosaur

Mary Ann
finding
dinosaurs
dinosaur's
mountain
113. pulled
covering
sunlight
114. airplane
shook
cross
afraid
worried
115. Mary Ann's
keep
Tutt
116. feed
Dandy
feeding
117. airplanes
118. trains
covered
more
wrong
famous
scientist
Dr. St. George
119. Dandy's
120. few
gym
band
121. quieted
122. wind
125. ago
these
biggest
taller
than
floors
126. meat
fighters

*killed*
Tyrannosaurus
*feet*
*tall*
*arms*
127. Brontosaurus
four
Corythosaurus
128. *parts*
died
change
colder
*bones*
Montana
Wyoming
Pennsylvania
New Mexico
together
skeletons
132. scary
134. Marvin's
*round*
*manhole*
Marvin
*covers*
*pipes*
135. *stay*
might
136. baseball
*bat*
*hit*
bread
137. prisoners
trapped
he'd
*teach*
139. *doorways*
ladder
*darker*
143. *cage*
146. strange

147. Betty Rubin
Lou's
birthday
*Lou*
collect
*rocks*
Mr. Konivi
*policeman*
*missing*
148. smile
Mr. Burt
*tag*
also
*bills*
*tags*
149. *smiled*
*thinking*
150. *smiles*
152. *jade*
*than*
worth
153. *should*
*collects*
156. yard
once
*hide*
159. stolen
*hides*
*Betty's*
*police*
*Rubin's*
160. we've
*bill*
*he'll*
161. *nearby*
*stayed*
*indoors*
*outdoors*
162. *policemen*
*policeman's*

left
Rubins'
167. Tammy
camps
*Rocky Mountains*
Terry
*Long's*
Peak
already
*noonday*
storm
168. *ready*
*pack*
camera
169. *camp*
*camping*
*trail*
behind
170. *stream*
*turn*
171. *side*
172. *squirrels*
173. chasm
lunch
174. minutes
*waterfall*
*started*
175. ahead
177. *handed*
*dry*
178. *inside*
179. *Tammy's*
rainbow
*slid*
*rest*
182. *rope*
*pull*
183. *faster*
*holding*
184. tight
186. *rested*

*safe*
188. potter
dear
himself
*such*
189. surprised
*ride*
190. *potter's*
*wife*
191. end
192. *land*
193. army
*fight*
*lead*
194. *king's*
*does*
enemy
195. *enemy's*
pony
horse
*smaller*
196. charger
197. *rides*
198. *quick*
199. charge
through
200. *picking*
*killed*
202. *riding*
*horses*
203. *letting*
204. *deed*
*yours*
208. Lisa's
*Lisa*
*climbing*
party
209. horrible
shy
210. answer

211. telephone
*tapped*
*filled*
question
*outside*
212. sandwich
213. *shyly*
216. music
Mozart
*Mozarts*
Wolfgang
Nannerl
years
217. *older*
wrote
218. act
*kiss*
219. *Wolfgang's*
220. Marie Antoinette
marry

227. corner
*crane*
*yelling*
*workmen*
remembered
229. wagon
231. watched
233. *ants*
*sidewalk*
*watch*
*hadn't*
235. *Dad*
*Ted*
*Tim's*
237. *daylight*
*daytime*
*bet*
*anymore*
242. Do-re-mi
Midori

English
kimono
243. United States
felt
*seen*
*class*
244. voice
*rang*
pretty
*bell*
*friendly*
hoped
245. *hers*
Renee
*Midori's*
building
burned
lost
246. better
carefully

obi
*sash*
247. *classroom*
*quickly*
*Renee's*
*note*
*hope*
signed
248. *lovely*
*dolls*
Maria
*children's*
*papers*
249. *doll's*
dress
*remember*
writing
*paper*
250. *calling*
you'd
*weren't*